Lucy Ellen Guernsey

The Twin Roses and How They Were Trained

Lucy Ellen Guernsey

The Twin Roses and How They Were Trained

ISBN/EAN: 9783744692786

Printed in Europe, USA, Canada, Australia, Japan

Cover: Foto ©ninafisch / pixelio.de

More available books at **www.hansebooks.com**

"You have ruined mamma's pretty vase." p. 105.

THE TWIN ROSES,

AND

How they were Trained.

BY THE AUTHOR OF
"IRISH AMY," "NELLY, OR THE BEST INHERITANCE," &c.

PHILADELPHIA:
AMERICAN SUNDAY-SCHOOL UNION,
No. 1122 Chestnut Street.

NEW YORK: 599 BROADWAY.

CONTENTS.

	PAGE
Chap. I.—A Hasty Promise	7
II.—The Babies	35
III.—The Rose Transplanted	61
IV.—Miss Brown	82
V.—Misunderstanding	101
VI.—The Breach Widens	126
VII.—Nelly	140
VIII.—Death	158
IX.—Farther Changes	178
X.—Rosy's Secret	196
XI.—An Unwelcome Visitor	214
XII.—A Contest	228

CONTENTS.

	PAGE
Chap. XIII.—Kitty	240
XIV.—Miss Brown	261
XV.—Becky	278
XVI.—Kitty	290
XVII.—The Meeting	303
XVIII.—Reunion	316

THE TWIN ROSES,

AND

HOW THEY WERE TRAINED.

CHAPTER I.

A HASTY PROMISE.

"IS Mrs. Mark at home?" asked Mrs. John Campion, hastily, as she shook the snow from her skirts on the steps of her sister-in-law's house, and then, anticipating the servant's reply, she exclaimed, in a tone of vexation, "You don't mean to say that she has gone out this horrible evening! I made sure of finding her at home; and I want to see her *so* much!"

"She a'n't gone far," said the woman who had opened the door, and who seemed rather inclined to resent Mrs. Campion's remark. "She only went across the common to carry something to old Miss Brown. We had some venison stew for dinner, and she thought maybe the old women might relish it, as she hain't had no appetite to speak of lately, and her folks don't know how to cook, no more than the pigs. If you want to see her very much, you'd better come in and wait; for she won't be long, I'm sure."

"Just as likely as not she will stay all the evening," said Mrs. Campion. "When Miss Brown gets going on the subject of her feelings and complaints, she never knows when to stop."

"She don't get a chance to get going very often: may-be that's the reason," replied Rebecca, between whom and Mrs. Campion there seemed to exist a sort of antagonism. "She never can say a word to her own folks without being snapped up. If ever the curse of ingratitude fell upon any one, it will fall upon Martha James and her husband, for the way they treat that old lady. But you'd better come in; for here comes Mrs. Campion this minute."

"Good-evening, Anne," said an alert little woman, entering the porch as Becky spoke, and making sundry energetic movements to get rid of the clinging snow. "Isn't this a storm? But why does Becky keep you standing at the door?"

"Because she couldn't make up her mind whether she wanted to come in or not," said Becky, answering for herself, as she retreated to her own domain. "I suppose she can decide, now you have come."

"What upon earth have you there, Veronica?" asked Anne. Her sister-in-law carefully unfolded her shawl, and displayed a small black kitten cuddled up in her arms. "Well, I declare! What a prize! A present, I suppose, from old Miss Brown."

"No," said Veronica. "Poor Miss Brown has not even a cat of her own to give away. This little thing I found astray upon the common, and it mewed at me so piteously, and purred so joyously when I took it up, that I had not the heart to abandon it in the snow-storm."

"Well, never mind that now. I want to talk to you about something more important than kittens."

"In one minute," said Veronica. "Just take off your bonnet and make yourself comfortable, while I find some milk for this poor little thing. I am sure it is half starved."

Anne made an impatient gesture, but followed her sister's advice, and settled herself in a comfortable arm-chair, while Veronica provided a saucerful of warm milk for the kitten, which it lapped with immense enjoyment. Veronica now produced her knitting, and, settling herself in the other arm-chair, waited for her sister-in-law's communication,—not, it must be confessed, with any appearance of absorbing interest. She knew how often Anne's mountains produced the very smallest of mice; and she expected nothing larger on the present occasion.

"Veronica, do you remember Daisy Birch, who was at school with us in T——?" asked Anne.

"Little Daisy Birch! Yes, certainly. She roomed with Addy Brush, and afterwards married her brother. An idle little thing she was, always in some scrape or other, but very pleasant and lively. What of her?"

"Veronica, Daisy Birch is dying in the Sisters' Hospital at this minute!"

"Why, Anne! Daisy Birch!" exclaimed Veronica, effectually roused, and dropping her knitting. "Are you sure? Who told you?"

"I have seen her this very day, Veronica. I should say she could not last twenty-four hours. The nurse says she may live a week or two; but it does not seem possible."

"They have a great deal of experience, you know," remarked Veronica. "But Daisy Birch! Poor little thing! How could it happen?"

"Very easily," replied Anne. "She has been living down in New Orleans, and had come as far as this place, on her way to New England, where, it seems, she has some friends, who she hoped might take care of her children; for she has twin babies about ten months old,—dear, rosy little girls as I ever saw. Well, it seems that somewhere on the road she met a person from her native place, who told her that the old aunt, or whoever it was she intended to go to, was dead, and there was no one of her father's family left in the place. Perhaps the shock was too much for her: at any rate, she was taken very ill at the hotel here, and the landlord, not knowing what else to do, sent her to the hospital, babies and all. It was by the merest chance that I found her. I went up to the hospital to carry some money

I had been owing old Mrs. Sweeny, our washerwoman, who has been there this long time with her leg, you know."

"I know," said Veronica. "I have been to see her a number of times."

"You never told me," said Anne. "You might have done my errand as well as not. But, however, I went into the wrong ward, by mistake, and there was this poor little woman sitting bolstered up in bed,—for it seems she cannot lie down,—with her babies beside her. She knew me in a minute, and called me by name; but I did not recognize her in the least till she told me who she was. You never saw any one so changed. Her hair is as gray as Miss Brown's."

"She used to have such superb chestnut hair," said Veronica. "I don't think I ever saw more beautiful hair. And she must be young, too. She cannot be nearly thirty. But did you hear any thing of her circumstances? Is she poor?"

"She says she has hardly a cent in the world. You know she made a runaway match."

"I know there was some trouble or other about her marriage. I remember I took a great dislike to John Brush, the only time I ever saw him,—partly, perhaps, because he was Addy's brother; though I know he had the reputation of being *fast* even then."

"Well, it was a runaway match, as I said. Daisy was an orphan, and a good deal of an heiress. Addy got the credit of cooking up the business, and I dare say she had a hand in it. Daisy's guardian refused his consent; but, as the property was all her own, of course he had no control over her. I heard of them a few years ago, boarding at the St. Charles in New Orleans, and making a great dash. It appears that Mr. Brush was killed in a duel about three months before these babies were born, and when the affairs came to be examined, there was nothing left of Daisy's property. All had been spent or wasted, and she was literally destitute.

"Her money and jewels were taken to pay their bill at the hotel. Finally, Addie took her into her house, till after her babies were born, and then coolly told her she would be obliged to provide for herself, and advised her to set up a school."

"Fancy Daisy teaching school!" exclaimed Veronica.

"Fancy any woman teaching school with

twin babies only three months old, and nobody but herself to take care of them!" said **Anne.**

"**But** Daisy Birch, above all! Why, she **was the** greatest dunce in the school. I don't believe she was off the roll half a dozen times **in** the whole three **years** I spent at T——; and then it was only on the days when I was monitress, and because I used regularly **to** catch her and put her in her right place before I rang the bell. She had fine musical talents, I remember, and she did use to practise industriously."

"It was her music which helped her at last," said Anne. "Some clergyman interested himself **and** found her a place in a church-choir, where she received a pretty good salary; and then she took pupils. But her strength soon gave out. She was attacked with **a** cough, and used to have slight turns of bleeding at the lungs whenever she sang. **At last** she had a severe attack, which laid her up entirely, and the physician said there was no hope of her ever being able to sing again. It **was** then she formed the resolution of coming North to find her father's friend; and the clergyman who had befriended her at first, got up a purse for her and paid her passage up the river. **But** she was sick two or three times upon the road, and she thinks some of her money was stolen. At any rate, she has only three dollars left, and the children are likely to go to the poor-house, for aught I see. That is what I came to tell you about. I told Daisy at once that I would take one of the children and bring it up for my own, and that you would adopt the other. And I want you to go up to the hospital the first thing in the morning and confirm my promise, that the poor thing's mind may be entirely at ease."

A flush of something like indignation rose in Veronica's face, and it seemed for a moment that she could not trust herself to speak; for she bent her eyes steadfastly on her work, and plied her needle busily for some moments before she answered. At last she said, calmly, though without looking up,—

"I don't think you should have said such a thing in my name without consulting me. It is a very serious matter to take a child in that way."

"Well, I declare!" exclaimed Anne, flushing in her turn. "If I had supposed you stood so extremely on your dignity, Veronica, I am sure I would not have ventured to use your name. I did not know you thought yourself such a grand person."

"It is not that I stand on my dignity, Anne; though I must say I do not relish having promises made in my name without my knowledge," returned Veronica. "But it is, as I said just now, a very serious matter to adopt a child. It is taking upon oneself a great responsibility."

"You were ready enough to patronize that miserable scarecrow of a cat," said Anne, looking at the new-comer, which was purring on the rug before the fire. "You would take in a hippopotamus if it should come and purr at you; but you care nothing for a poor orphan child."

"I should dearly love to hear a hippopotamus purr!" said Veronica, laughing.

"It is no laughing-matter," said Anne, indignantly. "There I left poor Daisy with her mind so relieved and settled; and now I must go to-morrow and tell her that she must leave the poor baby to charity, for you won't take it, after all. I thought better of you, Veronica; I did, indeed."

"You will please say nothing further in my name, either one way or the other, until I give you authority," said Veronica, decidedly. "If poor Daisy is disappointed, the fault is yours, not mine; for you had no right to make such a promise. Moreover, I have not yet said that I would not take the child. I must have time to think, and to consult my husband. You must see yourself that there is a great difference between taking in a stray kitten and adopting a baby to bring up as one's own. The kitten needs no care beyond food and lodging and kind treatment; but the child, if it lives, requires not only food and clothing, but discipline and education, both moral and mental. It is an immortal being, to be trained for immortality."

"But that is so much the more reason for its having a good home, Veronica," remarked Anne, in rather a subdued tone.

"True; and it is also a reason why the charge should not be undertaken lightly or unadvisedly, but soberly, reverently, discreetly, and in the fear of God. Moreover, it is a thing which, once being done, cannot be undone. If my kitten is troublesome, I can shut it out in the wood-house; or, if worse comes to worst, I can have it drowned. Even if my mythical hippopotamus should become a burden, I could probably sell him to the circus-people. But if I take a baby, I cannot cast it off in that way. I must keep it however it turns out,—whether it grows up healthy and handsome or diseased and deformed, good and dutiful or altogether the reverse."

"You might send it to the orphan-asylum, for that matter," said Anne.

"Hardly, I think. If the child goes to the asylum now, it will never remember any thing different, and will look forward to any change as an improvement; but to bring it up as your own, petted and indulged as the only child is sure to be, until it is old enough to think and remember and make comparisons, and then turn it over to a public charity, would be an extreme of cruelty hardly to be justified under any circumstances."

Anne fidgeted, and blushed a little. The truth was that, in the little thought she had bestowed upon the matter, she had finally ended all with, "And, after all, if the child turns out badly, I have only to send it to the asylum at last, instead of at first."

She changed her ground a little.

"I suppose you think it would give you a great deal of trouble?"

"As to that, I am not apt to mind trouble, and I am used to children, and like them. No, I did not reckon the trouble; though a child of that age nearly doubles the work of a household like ours. But Becky does not mind work, and she is fond of children. As to the expense, I think we might afford it well enough, since Mark has an increase of income, and we are entirely out of debt."

"John told me that this new arrangement would be a fine thing for Mark," observed Anne. "I am surprised to see you still at work for Mrs. Kirkland. I hoped at least you would give that up," she added, glancing at her sister's work,—a very delicate and beautiful piece of knitting.

"As to that, I had long ago promised to fill this particular order for Mrs. Kirkland, and I did not think it would be fair to disappoint her. But I do not see why I should give up my fancy-work, Anne. It is a pretty and pleasant occupation, and fills up many late evening-hours when Mark must be away and I can neither read nor sew. It makes, too, a very nice little addition to my private purse. No; I do not think I shall give it up just at present."

"Well, you are certainly two of the oddest people, you and Mark! But you have always taken your own way, and I suppose you always will," added Anne, in a tone of virtuous resignation: "so there is no use in talking about that. I do wish, though, that you would make up your mind about this baby. You put me in a very painful position if you refuse; though I suppose you will say it is my own fault. But I did feel so sure. I thought you would snatch at the chance."

"And so I should, my dear sister. If I were to consult my own inclination alone, I should say at once that I would take the child; but it is this very fact that makes me desirous to see the thing upon all sides. Our house has been very lonely the last year," said Veronica, her eyes filling with tears as she looked at the little chair which stood in the corner,—"more lonely than you could think, unless you had suffered the same experience that we have. You have never had any children in your house; and you cannot imagine the vacancy——"

"I beg your pardon, Veronica," said Anne, as her sister paused and busied herself with her knitting. "I am sure you mean to do what is right. Only, I am always in such a hurry to have things settled, and I felt so sorry for Daisy, and this plan looks so plain and easy. But when do you think you can decide?"

"I will try to let you know to-morrow, or the next day at farthest. And now tell me more about poor Daisy. Does she seem comfortable?"

"As much so as she can be—poor thing!—in the common ward of a hospital. The nurse seemed very kind; and Daisy told me herself that she had every attention."

"In the common ward!" repeated Veronica. "Surely, Anne, her condition might be improved in that respect. There are private rooms at the hospital, I know; and she might have one, if anybody would be answerable for the expense. I think we might undertake that between us for the little time she is likely to live. It is only four or five dollars a week. I cannot bear to think of the poor thing having no privacy for herself or her children."

"To be sure it would be a great deal better. I never thought of that," said Anne. "Of course I will bear my share of the expense. The ward is quiet enough, to be sure; but it is not like having a room to oneself, after all."

"Does Daisy seem aware of her own condition?"

"Oh, yes. She says she felt her doom was sealed when she left New Orleans, and—There! she wants very much to see a clergyman, and I promised to send Dr. Courtland up to her directly. I forgot all about it till this minute. What shall I do?"

"Cannot you send Harry?"

"Harry has gone home, and John is at some committee-meeting or other. It will have to wait till morning."

"And she may die in the mean time," said Veronica. "It is not late, Anne, and the storm is over. Suppose you go round to the doctor's with me? If he receives the message to-night, he can take the next car and go up at once. I am sure he will do so, under the circumstances."

"Why, it is terribly snowy," said Anne, hesitating, "and it makes my walk so much the longer. I did tell Daisy I would send him to-night; but I don't suppose it will make much difference."

"For shame, Anne!" said Veronica, indignantly. "Would you neglect the request of a dying woman, and such a request? Daisy may die during the night, or she may be too far gone to see the doctor in the morning."

"Oh, I will go. You need not put on that injured-air, Veronica, because I rather objected to walking half a mile in the snow, after being out all the afternoon. But you do love to make out that all your fellow-creatures are miserable sinners."

Veronica made no reply, knowing that the beginning of strife, especially with Mrs. John Campion, was like the letting out of water; and the sisters-in-law were soon on their way to the parsonage. The doctor had just come in from a long walk, and, in the luxury of dressing-gown, slippers, and a new book, was basking in the light of a coal fire. He sighed deep and long as he heard Anne's errand, and looked first at the fire and then at his boots and great-coat.

"I will go, of course," said he; "but I wish I had heard of it before. I was making a visit in that part of the town not an hour ago."

Anne felt a little conscience-stricken, but she made no remark; and the sisters presently separated, and returned each to her own fire-side.

Veronica put away her hood and shawl, and

seated herself once more by her bright fire. The room was not large, and was very simply furnished, but there was an aspect of comfort and elegance about it which is often wanting in apartments of more pretensions. The furniture was of chintz, which had evidently seen some service, though it was whole and clean. The paper was of a pretty sea-weed pattern in pale buff, and made a good background for the three or four good prints and the one beautiful oil landscape, the pride of Mark Campion's heart, which adorned the walls. The corners were furnished with shelves, which were filled—nay, crowded—with books, new and old, with magazines and papers; and on two or three beautifully carved brackets were placed plaster casts and an antique vase. These brackets were the work of Mark's own hands, the amusement of many a long winter's evening, and had cost Anne a great deal of wonder as to how Veronica could endure to have such a litter about her sitting-room. A basket work-table stood near the chimney-corner, piled up with the bright-coloured wools used by Veronica in her fancy-work,—another subject of wonder to Anne, who thought if Veronica must do such things she might at least keep them out of sight. Indeed, Anne was in the habit of bestowing so much wonder, advice, and reproof upon her sister-in-law and her concerns that it is no matter of surprise that Veronica sometimes became a little impatient, and that Becky openly expressed the wish that Mrs. John Campion would mind her own business.

Veronica took her work once more; but she plied her needle slowly, and often let it fall upon her lap, as she gazed thoughtfully at the fire. At last she rose, and, taking a candle from the mantel-piece, she lighted it and passed into an adjoining bedroom. Taking a key from her dressing-case, she opened a locked drawer, and sat thoughtfully gazing into it. The contents were not such as would have seemed to a stranger worth locking up. There were little, half-worn frocks and aprons, rows of neatly-folded socks, two or three pairs of little shoes, a broken doll, and some other playthings.

Veronica leaned her head on the drawer and wept bitterly for some moments. Then, seemingly controlling herself by a great effort, she dried her eyes, and proceeded to take out one garment after another from the drawer, and look it over. Finally, as with a sudden impulse, she laid them back, and locked them up once more.

"I cannot do that," said she to herself. "I would rather work my fingers off than see another child wearing my Anne's clothes."

The sound of a latch-key in the front door now announced an arrival, and, hastily restoring the key of the drawer to its place, she smoothed her hair and went to meet her husband. Mr. Mark Campion was a tall, strongly-made person, light-haired and yellow-bearded, with a pair of bright, dancing blue eyes, and a wonderfully guileless childlike expression for a grown man. He lifted his little wife from the ground, and gave her as hearty a kiss as if they had been separated for months instead of for hours.

"Tired, little woman?" he asked, tenderly. "You have had a long evening here alone. I thought I should never get away. Such a lot of people coming and bothering! and last of all, just as I thought myself released, comes little Wicks, in a towering rage about the misprints in his last article. However, I made short work of him:—sent him home to get sober."

"Is he drinking again?" asked Veronica.

"Very badly, I should say. He won't last long, at that rate. I pity his poor family; for he is a devil under the influence of brandy, though amiable enough at other times. But what has troubled my little woman?" added Mark, gently. "Now, there is no use in any denials. These eyes witness against you."

"Nothing,—at least, nothing new," said Veronica: "I had occasion to look into Anne's drawer," she added, in a lower tone. Her husband only answered by another kiss and a closer caress. Mr. Mark Campion, though he usually talked a great deal, was a man who knew when to be silent.

"But you have had no supper, and not much dinner," said Veronica, presently, rousing herself. "You must be very hungry. Becky," she added, as that discreet damsel opened the door, "Mr. Campion has had no supper."

"Well, I know that," returned Becky, who generally resented as an imputation any attempt to give her information respecting household matters. "I knew he would come home hungry as a bear; and so I just warmed up the stew that was left, and made some cocoa. You won't be the worse for a cup yourself, Mrs.

Mark, after tramping about in the cold and snow."

"You don't mean to say you have been out in this storm?" said Mark. "What possessed you?"

"I have not been far, I will tell you all about it presently," replied Veronica. "Come, wash your hands, and eat your supper while it's hot."

"Here is an encouragement to dissipation, now," said Mark, seating himself before the inviting tray which Becky brought in. "Such a supper is enough to tempt a man to stay out till eleven o'clock every night of his life."

"Ah, but you are not to suppose that you will have such a supper every night," said Veronica, as she poured out his cocoa. "Besides, don't you know Dr. Woodman says people who eat suppers invariably go to destruction?"

"He should make a special exception in favour of proof-readers, sub-editors, and literary hacks in general," remarked Mark, making a vigorous attack upon the provisions before him.

"Ah, it is all very well for you to call yourself a literary hack," said Veronica, laughing. "It would not do for anybody else."

"Very likely, my dear. We call ourselves miserable sinners every day, but we don't like other people to call us so."

"Well, and there is some reason in it, too," remarked Veronica. "One does not like meddling. I see a good many faults in my own household management every day, but I don't like to have Anne looking into my pantry and telling me I ought to be ashamed to keep my sitting-room in such a litter."

"You don't seem to mind it at all when my mother gives you hints about housekeeping," said Mark. "I saw you listening and looking as if she had been an oracle, while she was showing you how to cook that bit of venison you were going to throw away as useless."

"That is quite another matter. Your mother has every right to advise, and she always does so in a gentle and ladylike way. I never saw any one more delicate about interference than she is. I only wish she had stayed over till to-day."

"Why, what new emergency has come up? Has Zuzu got the apoplexy from over-feeding, or are you thinking of taking a cat upon trial?"

"Something a great deal more serious than either," replied Veronica. "Something I wish to talk over with you when you have finished your supper. As for Zu's apoplexy, I think it would be, as Becky's mother said about the gosling, a happy release; and as to the cat, it has taken me, as you see," she added, pointing to the little purring heap upon the hearth-rug. "But this is really a grave matter,—something which, once being done, cannot be undone."

Mark saw that his wife was in earnest, and, settling himself in his favourite arm-chair and taking the cat on his knee, he proceeded to give his undivided attention while Veronica related her conversation with her sister-in-law and the events which gave rise to it. When she had finished, she looked anxiously at her husband for his opinion, which he did not seem in a hurry to give. He sat for some time smoothing the kitten's fur and looking thoughtfully at the fire. At last he said,—

"I wonder whether any woman in the world but Anne would have done such a thing. I wonder if she even thought of consulting John before she promised to take the child herself."

"I dare say not," replied Veronica. "It

would have been only a form, at any rate; for he never contradicts her in any fancy."

"Still, the observance of forms sometimes saves a good deal of trouble," returned Mark; "and even John now and then rebels. She would be in a pretty predicament if he should refuse to take the child, after all. But we know Anne and her ways too well to be surprised at any eccentricities of hers. So we will put her out of the question." He sat silent a while longer, and seemed in danger of drifting into one of his customary brown studies, when a small scratch from the kitten aroused him.

"Well," said he, "it is a serious matter, as you say. What do you think about it?"

"I should like it very much, if you see no objection," said Veronica, simply and gravely, but with a flush upon her cheeks and a suffusion of her gray eyes which showed how near the subject was to her heart.

Mark looked earnestly at her.

"You are sure you would like it?"

"Quite sure."

"A child of that age would make you a good deal of trouble and anxiety. Are the children healthy?"

"So Anne says—no, I do not think she said any thing about that, directly. She said they were rosy and pretty."

"Then I dare say they are healthy as well."

"And, if they are not, they have so much the more need of care," said Veronica.

"True, little wife; but it is your health I must think of."

"But you know I am very strong, Mark. I believe I have gone over all the objections in my own mind a dozen times," continued Veronica. "I am so afraid of being misled by my inclinations."

"Well, what are the objections?" asked Mark. "Let us have them in detail."

"First, there is the expense."

"That need be no great matter for some years to come," said Mark; "and meantime we are growing more and more able to meet it. I do not suppose we shall have any thing to leave her; but we must give her a thoroughly good education, and thus enable her to maintain herself if it should become necessary. Well, what next?"

"Then, there is the responsibility, Mark."

"True; and that is, no doubt, very great.

But it would be no more for this little one than for a child of our own; and if we find it too much for our strength, we must cast our burden upon Him who has promised to help the heavy-laden. We must remember, Veronica, that we cannot *make* the child, and we are not expected to do so. All we have in our power is to act according to our best light, both for its bodily and spiritual welfare, and leave the rest to God."

"Then, you know, Mark, if we take the child, we must keep it always, however it turns out. It may be sickly, or ill-disposed, crooked in mind or body; and yet, having once adopted it, we cannot cast it off."

"Of that we must take our chance with any child, as much with our own as with a stranger's. But we will pray upon it and sleep upon it, my dear, and then decide; though, honestly, I believe we have in our own minds decided already."

Veronica smiled. She thought so too.

"It will make the house very lively again," continued Mark, in a musing tone. "I fear you have found it desolate enough for the last few months, Veronica, with only me for company."

c

"Are you not better to me than ten sons?" said Veronica. Her husband looked at her with something shining very brightly in his blue eyes; but he did not make her any answer in words.

CHAPTER II.

THE BABIES.

VERONICA rose early the next morning, and before her husband made his appearance she had dusted the sitting-room, arranged Mark's desk and books, which were apt to fall into dire confusion, and held a consultation with Becky upon various household matters. Becky was a strong-armed, somewhat hard-featured woman, who might have been of any age from thirty to fifty. She had been taken from the poor-house as a "bound-girl" by Mark Campion's mother, and had remained in the family many years. When Mrs. Campion gave up housekeeping on Mark's marriage, Becky came to live with Veronica, and had stayed with her ever since, the only servant through some years of hard toil and trial. She was an excellent cook and laundress, perfectly faithful, active, trustworthy, and, in spite of a somewhat crabbed manner, singularly even-tempered. When Mrs. John Campion married, she was anxious to secure Becky's services; and, not having been brought up with any strict ideas of her duty towards her neighbour, she offered Becky nearly double wages and a great increase of dignity if she would accept the post of housekeeper. Becky, however, treated with the utmost scorn the notion that she should "better herself" in any such way.

"Live with Anne Holley, indeed," she said to Mrs. Campion. "I'd as soon live with a whole nest of squirrels! Keep house, indeed! It would be a large house that would keep her and me at the same time. If Mr. John is going to make a fool of himself, *I* a'n't."

"You should not speak so of my son's wife, Rebecca," said Mrs. Campion. "Mr. John has a right to please himself."

"And I've got a right to please myself," returned Becky; and there the matter ended.

Anne Campion was not possessed of much delicacy, and she was firmly persuaded in her own mind of her infinite superiority to Veronica, especially in all matters of housekeeping. Veronica, she argued, was a literary woman:

literary women never made good housekeepers: *ergo*, Veronica was not a good housekeeper. Consequently, she had not the slightest hesitation in advising, criticizing, and even reproving her elder sister-in-law. Her comments always roused Becky's ire to the utmost, and she never failed to express her opinions on such occasions; and there was a sort of guerilla warfare kept up between them, which was sometimes amusing and sometimes rather annoying. It was enough that any project originated with Mrs. John to set Becky against it; and Veronica saw that this circumstance might be a difficulty in the way of Becky's taking kindly to the baby. She therefore, in unfolding her plan, wisely kept Mrs. John in the background. Becky loved children dearly, and she had mourned deeply for the two little ones who had been removed. She approved of the plan at once, and cheerfully promised to take her share of the trouble entailed by the new baby.

"It will seem very nice to have a little one about the house once more," said she. "And who is to take the other,—poor little dear?"

"Mrs. John means to take the other herself," replied Veronica.

"Mrs. John!" exclaimed Becky, in a tone which spoke volumes.

"Yes," replied Veronica. "It was she who proposed the plan in the first place. She found poor Mrs. Brush at the hospital, and came immediately to tell me."

"Oh, it is all right, I dare say," said Becky, beginning to chop energetically. "Only I pity the poor child: that's all."

"Becky, you are prejudiced against Mrs. John," said Veronica, gravely. "Nothing that she could do would be right in your eyes. I do not think you ought to allow yourself to be governed by such feelings."

"She is so aggravating," said Becky,—"always interfering, and directing folks old enough to be her mother. When I was young, folks were taught not to reprove their elders. And, after all," she continued, "there does not seem to be much comfort in bringing up other folks' children. Look at poor old Miss Brown. Nobody could do more for an own child than she did for Martha James. She denied herself decent clothes and food that the child might have all she wanted,—might go to a good school, and dress like other girls. She worked for her night and day, and indulged her in every thing; and see what has come of it. Some people say that adopted children always turn out badly."

"I do not think spoiled children are apt to be grateful to those who spoil them, under any circumstances," said Veronica, suppressing a smile at the sudden change which had come over Becky's sentiments at the mention of Mrs. John. "I think Miss Brown made a great mistake in putting all her property into the hands of Martha and her husband, thus rendering herself dependent upon them."

"That doesn't excuse them for treating her so," said Becky, shortly. "It only makes them worse."

"Nothing can excuse such conduct as theirs," said Veronica. "But, Becky, I can think of another instance where a poor child was taken into a family, in which she remained more than thirty years, repaying ten times over, by her faithful friendship and her unwearied services, all that had been done for her."

"Do you mean me?" asked Becky. "Bless you, my dear, I haven't done any thing,—only earned my wages. I do think I have done that."

"You have done a great deal more than

that, Becky. No mere servant could have helped me through my seasons of severe trial as you did. It seems to me that I could never have lived through Anne's last sickness without you."

"Now, *don't*, Mrs. Mark," said Becky; "as if I wouldn't have laid down my life for either of them sweet lambs any minute, to say nothing of you and Mr. Mark. Besides, didn't you nurse me with my broken leg as though I had been your own sister, scrimping yourselves every way to buy nice things for me, and keep a fire for me in the best room in the house? To be sure, Mrs. John came and sat up with me too," said Becky, relenting a little, "and took real good care of me: only she was sure to wake me up every time I dropped asleep, and kept up such a creaking and rustling and rattling that she nearly drove me crazy. But then she meant well,—poor thing! and if folks haven't got sense they haven't, and that is all about it. The apostle tells some people that they suffered fools gladly, seeing they themselves were wise; but I do think it takes a sight of wisdom to suffer some folks. And so she is going to take a child to bring up? Well, well!"

"I do not know what would become of the other baby if she did not take it," said Veronica. "I could hardly undertake two; and there are no family friends. I think she will be very kind. My only fear is lest she should be too kind."

"That's the way it will end, I expect," said Becky. "She will spoil the child till there is no living with it, and then turn it over to you. However, I won't borrow trouble about that. I wonder if the little dears have got any clothes?"

"I dare say they are not very well provided with them. The mother has been very poor ever since they were born; and, besides, coming as they do from New Orleans, they will not be likely to have any thing warm enough for this climate. I shall find out all about that to-day."

"There are those clothes of Anne's," said Becky, with some hesitation. "If you thought of using them, I might get them out and look them over."

"I do not feel as though I could use those things, Becky. It may be weak in me, but I don't think I could bear to see another child wearing those frocks."

"I suppose you have as much right to have feelings as other folks," said Becky.

"But there is that pretty blue merino Mrs. Campion gave me," continued Veronica. "If you have time to-day, I should like to have you rip it and press it **out**. I think I can make a couple of pretty frocks and a nice little cloak from the skirt."

"Of course I shall have time," replied Becky. "I haven't any thing to do, after I have washed my dishes and baked my pies and swept and dusted the parlour. And I guess, too, I had better set up some little woollen stockings. My knitting is all done, and Mr. Mark doesn't want any more socks just now."

"Very well: you will find some nice red and white yarn in the bottom of my basket."

"I calculate to buy the yarn myself," said Becky, shortly. "If I choose to spend some of my own money on the child, I don't see why you need object, Mrs. Mark."

"Certainly not, Becky: please yourself," replied Veronica, smiling, and perceiving that the baby's place was already secured in Becky's heart. "But now we will have prayers. I hear Mr. Mark in **the** dining-room."

"What are you going to do to-day, Veronica?" asked Mark at the breakfast-table.

"I am going up to the hospital, to see poor Daisy and settle with the Sisters about letting her have a private room. I do not like to think of her being in the common ward, with all sorts of people. Anne has agreed to bear half the expense; for of course it will cost something."

"As she did of Julia Green's rent, eh?"

"Now, Mark, you need not bring that up. You know John paid Anne's share long ago. But this will be no more than a trifle in any case; for they say Daisy can only live a few days at the outside."

"You might bring her home with you," said Mark. "The front bedroom is warmed, at any rate; and Becky would enjoy having her to nurse."

"I do not suppose she can be moved so far. But are you sure you would be willing to take such a burden, Mark?"

"Why, as to that, it is no more than I should like to have some good Christian to do for you under like circumstances," replied Mark. "But act according to your own judgment, my dear. You are sure to be right."

And Mark really meant what he said; for, a dreamy, meditative sort of man himself, he had unbounded faith in his wife's practical wisdom.

Veronica soon despatched her household affairs,—indeed, Becky left her very little to do in that line,—and then proceeded to the hospital. Anne had agreed to meet her at half-past ten; but, when she arrived, no Anne had made her appearance. Veronica was not sorry. She wanted an opportunity for some private conversation with the hospital authorities and with Daisy herself. Daisy had had a restless night, and was somewhat weaker in consequence, the Sister said, but still she was comfortable, and it would do her no harm to talk a little, if she were not excited.

"Your friend means kindly," said she, "but she should learn to control herself if she means to visit sick people. Tears of sympathy are all very well in books, my dear; but it will never do to bestow them too freely upon people who are subject to coughing-fits."

"Was she able to see Dr. Courtland?" asked Veronica.

"Yes; and she seemed to enjoy his visit. She behaves wonderfully well —poor child!— all things considered."

Veronica mentioned Mark's wish that Daisy should be removed to their own house; but the Sister shook her head decidedly.

"It will never do. She would most likely die on the road. I am not sure it would answer even to remove her from one room to another."

"I am sorry to hear that," said Veronica. "I hoped we might at least secure a private room for her."

The Sister considered. "It will be a risk," she repeated. "Still, if the room were all ready and well warmed beforehand——Well, my dear, go in and see your friend, and I will talk to the doctor about the matter. If he consents, I will have the room all prepared before we say any thing to her about it. Then we can have her carried down at once, and she will have no time to get flurried."

"How much there is in knowing how!" thought Veronica, as she followed the Sister up the stairs and through the long, cleanly-scrubbed passage. "Not one person in ten would ever have thought of that."

She found poor Daisy half sitting up, supported in her little bed by piles of pillows, at one end of the large ward, in which there were only two or three other patients. Her skin was white as paper, though she had a round, red spot upon one cheek, and her large hazel eyes looked unnaturally clear and bright. The two babies were sitting on a coverlet placed upon the floor,—one peacefully sucking its thumb, the other playing with an extempore doll. They were very pretty children, not in the least alike,—one being dark with black eyes, and the other inheriting her poor mother's chestnut hair and transparent complexion.

Daisy recognized her friend directly, and held out her hand to her with a sweet smile. Veronica found it hard to follow the Sister's direction and preserve her calmness as she looked at her old school-mate.

"You are not in the least changed, Veronica," said she, regarding her fondly, after she was seated by the bedside. "I should have known you anywhere. You can hardly say as much for me, I suppose?"

"Your hair is gray, and that makes a difference," replied Veronica, "and your expression is a good deal changed, but still your smile is the same. You were a giddy little thing when I knew you, Daisy. Do you remember how I used to shut you into your room before I rang the study-bell, that I might not have to mark you for being out of place?"

"I remember how you used to help me with my lessons when no one else had the patience," replied Daisy; "only you would make me find the words and do the sums myself, and pin me down till I accomplished my task, instead of doing every thing for me. You were always one of the grave, practical pupils, Veronica."

"I was made so by circumstances," replied Veronica. "My cares came early upon me. I was five years older than you, too; and that makes all the difference at our ages."

"And I am young still:—I am only twenty-five," said Daisy, sighing. "Yet it seems as if I had had a long life already. If it were not for my poor babies, I should not desire to live any longer. But it seems hard to go and leave them to strangers!"

"You must not think you are leaving them to strangers, my child," observed the Sister, overhearing the remark. "In any event, you leave them to God; and surely He is no stranger."

"It was partly about the children that I

came to see you," said Veronica, when they were left to themselves. "You know I have no little ones left of my own, and Mark and I both thought we should like to take one of the babies and bring it up as our child. We are not rich, and probably never shall be; but we have a comfortable home, and are able to give the little one a good education, which, after all, is the best inheritance in this country. We will bring it up, as far as we are able, in **the fear of** God **and the** knowledge of **His** word. I cannot say more; but that much I may safely promise, both for Mark and myself."

Daisy drew a long breath, and leaned back on her pillows with a look of intense relief.

"I am deeply thankful, Veronica. I do trust you entirely. Anne said you would take the child; but I did not know. I did not dare to build upon it. I remembered Anne's old headlong way **of** making promises, and I could see that she was not much changed. The Sisters would have taken Rosy into their asylum. They have been very good to me, and I hope I am grateful; but I did not like to think of my Rosy growing up a Roman Catholic. You know, after all, if we think we are right we must think they are wrong," said Daisy, appealingly.

"Of course," replied Veronica. "We may reverence and love what is good and praiseworthy in people; but that does not make it necessary for us to adopt their errors. If an Arab should succour me with water in the desert, I should be deeply grateful to him; but I should not feel that I was obliged to believe in Mohammed on that account. Which of the children is Rosy?"

"The fair one. The other is Kitty,—named for Mr. Brush's mother and sister."

"And you would prefer to have me take Rosy?"

"Why, yes, I think so. You see, Veronica, she is like me, and I am afraid she inherits my own and my mother's constitution; and you are used to nursing. Besides, I know Anne likes Kitty best. She thinks the child is like her family."

"Say no more, my dear Daisy: I will gladly take Rosy. Indeed, I think Mark would prefer her, if he allowed himself to have any choice. He has an artist's admiration for chestnut hair."

"I am very thankful," said Daisy, with a

D

smile which was radiant with peace and satisfaction. "My precious babies will have good homes and kind friends when I am gone. God has been very good to me. I am sure He will take care of them." She lay with closed eyes and clasped hands for a few moments, and then, suddenly rousing herself, she spoke with energy:—

"Veronica, promise me one thing. Promise me, sacredly, that, whatever happens, my daughters shall never be turned over to Adela Brush. Send them to the asylum, bind them out to service in honest families,—any thing that is decent; but never, *never* put them into the power of that woman! Promise me, Veronica."

"I promise you that, so far as it is in my power to prevent it, she shall never have any thing to do with them," said Veronica. "Don't excite yourself, Daisy. But, my dear child," she added, with some hesitation, "whatever Adda has done, you must try to forgive her from your heart."

"I have tried, and I hope I have done so," said Daisy. "But you don't know what I have suffered. I never would have believed that any one could treat a sick person as she treated me. Such cold, deliberate, constant unkindness, shown in such mean little ways! For one instance: a lady gave me one of those books of texts, to hang upon the wall, you know:—I forget the name."

"The Silent Comforter," said Veronica.

"Yes. Well, I hung it at the foot of my bed, and turned over the leaves, or got one of the servants to turn over the leaves, every day; and it *was* a comforter,—about the only one I had in that house, except the poor coloured woman who waited on me. Well, one day Adela wanted a bit of paper to light the gas, and she deliberately tore one of the leaves out and used it, and then threw it into the fire. That is a specimen of her daily conduct. Then, if I complained of any thing, she taunted me with my ingratitude and dependence, and told me I had better go to the hospital. I am sure I would have gone in a minute, if I could. She used to tell me, over and over, that my husband's death was all owing to me,—that it was caused by my light conduct with gentlemen, and that my extravagance ruined him,—when we had not a cent which was not mine. Mr. Brush was not what he should have been, but he was kind to me, and I loved him dearly. He was sensible in his last hours, and prayed earnestly for forgiveness. That is my great comfort in thinking about him."

"It is the greatest comfort," said Veronica. "'The blood of Jesus Christ cleanseth from all sin;' and, 'To-day shalt thou be with me in paradise,' was spoken to one who repented at the eleventh hour. Yet those run a fearful risk who put off repentance and prayer to a death-bed."

"It was Adela who made the match," continued Daisy. "The affair began in school. He used to send me letters and presents by Adela, and I thought it a fine thing to have a secret and a lover,—though I did not care a pin for him at that time. Then, before I knew it, I was entangled in an engagement, and Adela threatened all sorts of things if I broke it off. She said I was entirely in her power; and I believed her. But I loved Mr. Brush afterwards. He was wild, and had no principle,—they were never brought up to have any,—but he was very kind to me, whatever he might have been out of my sight. I remember well that last morning. He went out before I was up, and he came back and kissed me twice. I wondered what was the matter; but I never guessed,—never thought of any harm, till they brought him in wounded."

"You are tiring yourself, Daisy," said Veronica. "Do not talk any more now."

"It does me good," said Daisy. "It is such a long, long time since I have had a friend to talk to!"

"What was the cause of the duel?" Veronica ventured to ask.

"Some gambling business. They quarrelled over cards, and struck one another, and after that there was nothing for it, according to their notions, but to fight. It was not what Adela said: I was foolish enough in many ways, but not in that. They don't think so much of human life there as we do here; but the affair made a great noise, and Mr. Brush was much blamed. Whatever his faults were, he repented seriously and sincerely, if ever any man did. He saw at that time how he had wasted his life and his talents. I think if he had lived he would have been very different; but it was not to be. He lingered some days, in great suffering both of body and mind; but he had peace at the last, and died with a prayer on his lips. After all, Veronica, it was drinking that did the mischief,—that, and the company to which it led. Oh, how many young men I saw go to utter destruction in the few years I lived in New Orleans!

"Mr. Brush knew his own danger, and often **declared** that he would never touch another drop; but he was always led away. If there were no one else to do it, Adela herself would lend a hand to the work, and laugh and sneer at him till he would take a glass just to get rid of her; and then, of course, all was over."

"I should think it incredible that a woman could act such a part, if I had not myself known such an instance," observed Veronica. "In this case it was a wife who led away her husband."

"It was more to torment me than any thing else, I do believe," continued Daisy. "She seemed to conceive an utter hatred **to** me as soon as I was married. But that is her nature. She can no **more** help it, apparently, than a kitten can help teasing **a** mouse. She drives her servants almost mad; and I should **not** wonder if there were a fearful tragedy acted in the house some day. I am deeply thankful that my children are not left in her power."

"I would not think of her more than I

could help, Daisy," said Veronica. "The more one dwells on such things, especially when one is weak, the worse they appear; one is tempted to act all the scenes over again, with variations and additions, till they are worse in the imagination than they were in the reality."

"They could not well be much worse," replied Daisy, shaking her head. "**But you are right, Veronica. It is not good to dwell on them.** I would rather think of the kindness I have received. A great many people were very good to me after I left Adela,—Mr. Fowler especially. He was the clergyman who found me a place to sing in church. Oh, Veronica, what a comfort it was to me! The first Sunday or two I did not enjoy the service very much. I had a feeling of responsibility and anxiety lest something should go wrong; but after that I used to look forward to Sunday as to a haven of rest. I could always forget my troubles when I was singing. My heart used to go up with the music. They said afterwards that singing was bad for me; but I know better. It kept me alive for a long time."

The attending Sister now appeared, to say that the room was ready; and Daisy, well wrapped up, was carefully lifted from the bed to an arm-chair, and transported thither with very little trouble. She bore the exertion better than had been expected, but seemed so tired when finally settled that Veronica thought it best to leave her. Having kissed her little nursling, and secured one of her frocks for a pattern, she went down-stairs, meeting Anne in the hall.

"Why, Veronica!" she exclaimed. "How long have you been here?"

"Since half-past ten. What has kept you so long?"

"Long! Why, it is only a quarter to one. I promised to be here at half-past twelve: didn't I?"

"Half-past ten, I understood. **Don't** you remember my saying that I should have to get up early to finish my work for Mrs. Kirkland?"

"**Did you?** Are you sure? I thought it **was half-past** twelve; but I don't imagine it makes much difference. I suppose I can go up and see Daisy directly?"

"I don't think I would go just now," said Veronica, detaining her. "Daisy has been talking a great deal, for her, and she has just been moved to her new room. The nurse has taken the babies out, and Daisy has composed herself to sleep. It will be better not to disturb her."

Anne looked vexed and disappointed. "I don't see what I am to do," said she. "I wanted to see her so very much. I thought I might take the child home to-day. I do so long to have her all to myself."

"I do not think Daisy would be willing," said her sister-in-law. "She seems to cling to them so closely, it would be cruelty to take them away till the last minute. She tells me that you have decided to take Kitty."

"Why, yes, I believe so. She looks more like me. All our family have black hair. I suppose it makes **very** little difference to you?"

"Very little," said Veronica, smiling. "Indeed, I think I should have chosen Rosy at any rate."

"Should you?" asked Anne. "Why?"

"Principally because Mark prefers light hair."

"To be sure, chestnut hair is more uncommon. I don't know but I should like it better myself," said Anne, considering. "But then Kitty has such rosy cheeks, and she looks stronger than her sister. I am sure I don't know what to say."

"I understood you had decided already," said Veronica. "But, if there is any question about the matter, Daisy's wishes ought to settle it; and she seemed particularly desirous that I should take Rosy. She thinks there may be danger of the child turning out delicate."

"Oh, if she is going to be sickly, I am sure I do not want her. Only, I think it is very ungrateful in Daisy to show such a distrust of me, when I was the first to propose taking the children at all. It does not look very well, I must say."

"I don't think it was any distrust on Daisy's part, Anne. It was only that she knew I had had more experience with children than yourself."

"Oh, well, it doesn't matter. It is the way of the world, anyhow. But what have you there?"

"One of Rosy's frocks. I must have some warm clothes made for her. I am sure she is not warmly enough dressed for this climate."

"I shall keep Kitty in white till she is three years old," said Anne, with decision. "Everybody does so."

"Everybody must have more time for sewing, washing, and ironing than we have at our house," said Veronica. "A child of that age will need three or four white frocks a week to keep her decent. But I must not stay to discuss the subject now. What did John say to your plan?"

"Oh, he consented easily enough: only he said, ·You must remember, Anne, it won't do to get tired of a live plaything and throw it away as you do a dead one.' I don't see why he should say so, I'm sure: only he likes to make remarks of that kind. What did Mark say?"

"He was very much pleased, as I foresaw he would be. He wanted to bring Daisy home at once to our own house; but the Sister says it will not do to move her."

"And you think it will not answer for me to take Kitty home to-day? However, perhaps it is just as well, for I want to furnish my nursery. Well, there is no use in my staying, if I cannot see Daisy. Shall I take you home?"

"No, thank you. I am going to walk part of the way, and make a call. Good-by."

On their way out, the sisters-in-law met

the nurse, with the two babies in her arms. It chanced that Rosy was crying and had **a** red nose, while Kitty was laughing merrily, —a circumstance which quite satisfied **Mrs.** John with her first choice.

CHAPTER III.

THE ROSE TRANSPLANTED.

CONTRARY to every one's expectation, Daisy lingered on for nearly two weeks longer. As her strength decayed, she suffered less, and had many days of comparative comfort. Veronica visited her frequently, spending many hours by her bedside, sometimes reading to her, sometimes sitting silently at work, or playing with the babies. Daisy was at times much inclined to talk over the experiences of her short life; and the nurse thought it would do no harm to indulge her. In this way Veronica learned more of her friend's real character than she had ever known while they were at school together. Daisy was fond of recurring to her school-days.

"What nice times we had at T——!" said she, one day, after they had been discussing old times in this way. "I never saw such a cheerful school as that was. So much pains seemed to be taken to make the girls happy."

"Yes; they were very pleasant days," replied Veronica. "Yet a great many girls used to complain bitterly of the fare and accommodations. Mrs. J. used to say the grumblers were generally those who had never lived half as well in their lives before. I know that was true in some cases,—those of Mary Draw and Julia Millener, for instance. I knew how they lived at home; and their complaints always seemed to me perfectly ridiculous."

"The worst of it was, not having a room to oneself, but being obliged to take just such a room-mate as happened to come along," remarked Daisy.

"That could hardly be helped, I suppose," said Veronica; "and, after all, people generally assorted themselves pretty soon. I always wondered, however, that you kept on with your room-mate as you did. I always thought her the most disagreeable girl in school."

"I don't know how it was, myself," replied Daisy; "only she made me afraid of her. She found out wrong things that I did, and used to threaten to betray me. She led me into scrapes and made me do what was wrong, and that gave her a handle over me. There was not a girl in the school who broke more rules, and not one who was more seldom found out, than **Adela.** Even Miss M., who saw through most of the girls, never thoroughly knew Adela, though I know she used to suspect her; but she never succeeded in catching her. But **I won't** talk about her. I should like to see **Mrs. W.** and Miss M., and all of them, once **more.** I should like to go through the old **halls,** and into the rooms, and have a good scolding from Mammy J., again. I dare say she would say that all my ill health was owing to my running out some time without my over-shoes."

"She might be right, too," observed Veronica. "I have no doubt that the seeds of ill health are often sown by early imprudence. Girls are so apt to be careless when they are away from home. We were well looked after, too, at Mrs. W.'s; but it would take a dozen Mrs. J.s to keep within bounds such a houseful of girls as we had at T——."

"I was careless, I know," said Daisy. "I never was brought up to have any care. I never did any thing I did not like, at home.

No duties were ever exacted of me. Mrs. Dale, my guardian's wife, used to say, 'Oh, well, it is a motherless child,—poor thing!' whenever Mr. Dale found fault, as he sometimes did, with my idleness. I am sure I don't know how I ever learned to read and write; for no one made me. They meant to be very kind; but I have sometimes doubted whether it was real kindness, after all."

"I very much doubt it," said Veronica. "I think the sooner children learn that they have duties to perform, the better for them and for every one else."

"I think so too. It comes so very hard when one is obliged to take them up; and they come to every one sooner or later, and in some shape or other. But Mrs. Dale was very good to me, and she did teach me some things, Veronica,—things which I never quite forgot, and which came back to me when I needed them most. I remember how she used to take me on her lap, the last thing before I went to bed, and sing to me the Cradle Hymn. The very first thing I noticed after my babies were born, was Chloe, the coloured woman who waited on me, singing, 'Hush, my dear, lie still and slumber,' to the babies. She was frightened when I burst out crying. I believe she thought she had killed me; but it did me all the good in the world. I had not been able to shed a tear since my husband died, except just at first, and my head burned like fire, while my heart seemed cold and dry as dust."

"Could not you pray, Daisy?" asked Veronica, softly.

"Not for a long time," said Daisy, shaking her head. "You see, I felt that I had been so much to blame. Not for my husband's death, but for other things. You know I lost my first baby."

"I did not know you ever had any but these," said Veronica.

"Yes: my first was a boy. It only lived ten days. Oh, how I did grieve for it! I had been pretty quiet for a good while before it was born, not through any good will of mine, but because the doctor was peremptory and I had to obey. Then, of course, I was obliged to think a little; and I grew more serious, read my Bible, and prayed,—and would have gone to church, only I was not able. There was an elderly lady in the house, who was very kind to me. She was very religious, and I learned a great deal of her. When my baby died, I was thoroughly sobered, and I made a great many resolutions. I did live very near to God for a long time, and I loved Him, Veronica,—I know I did,—and tried to please Him. Adela laughed at me and teased me; but Mr. Brush always took my part, and said I should do as I pleased. He did not care for such things himself, but I think he liked to see women religious."

"That is the case with a great many such men," said Veronica. "But go on, Daisy, if you are not tired. How did it all end?"

"I hardly know how I began to fall away," continued Daisy. "It began by small things at first. We lived with a wild, reckless set,—foreigners and Creoles,—who cared no more for Sunday than for any other day. They would go to the theatre or opera as soon on Sunday evening as any other; or, if they did not, they would play cards at home. I was led to do things that I knew to be wrong, and the old feelings and temper came back upon me. I used to resist feebly; but the resistance grew less and less, and the sins more and more, till I left off prayer almost entirely. My friend Mrs. Carter went away, and I had no one to turn to for advice or help; for I had not become acquainted with any clergyman. I was not happy all the time; but I was very gay. Once in a while I would make up my mind to do better; but my resolutions were soon overthrown, and at last I left off trying, and only endeavoured to keep myself from thinking all that I could.

"I was waked up with a terrible shock when my husband died. I saw all my sin and misery plainly enough then. A great gulf seemed to open at my feet, from which there was no escape. I could not cry; I could not pray; I could not repent. My poor husband prayed, and I tried to join him; but, Veronica, I could not. It seemed impossible —absolutely physically impossible—for me to utter a prayer."

"You are exciting yourself, Daisy," said Veronica.

"No: I want to tell you all about it, now I have begun. I never told anybody before. Well, this lasted till my babies were a week old; and I got no relief. Every thing seemed so hard and cold. Sometimes it even seemed to me that it was all a mistake together,—that there was no God, and no dear Jesus, after all,

—nothing but a waste and confused desolation. Oh, it was dreadful!"

"I should think so, indeed," said Veronica, shuddering. "How did you ever live through it?"

"I am sure I do not know. I suppose God strengthened me; though I did not see Him. At last, as I said, I heard Chloe singing to the baby, and that set me to crying. The tears were a great relief, physically. Chloe was frightened, and would have stopped singing, but I begged her to keep on, and to sing something else. She sang 'Rock of Ages,' to the same tune we used at school, and then a hymn, beginning—

'Come, humble sinner.'

"'That's the place to come to, Mrs. John,' said she, when she had finished: 'right to the foot of the cross,—right to Jesus.'

"'I can't, Chloe,' said I. 'I have tried, and I cannot. It is all dark to me. I cannot see his face anywhere.'

"'Then come in the dark, my lamb,' said the old woman. 'Call, and He will hear you.'

"'I cannot call,' I replied. 'I cannot pray.'

"'Then wait, without praying. Do any

thing but give up. Oh, honey, Jesus loves you! He loves you in all your sin and sorrow. Don't **ever** doubt that! Just see what your book says.' And she read from the 'Silent Comforter,' hanging upon the wall, slowly, and spelling the words,—for she knew very little, poor thing!—'He that spared not His own Son, but delivered Him up for us all, how shall He not with Him freely give us all things?' (Rom. viii. 32.)

"She was called away then, and I was left alone. I lay in a kind of dumb despair, unable to think, even to feel any thing but that I was utterly miserable and hopeless. All at once something seemed to say to me, 'How much must you have loved any one before you could give up the life of one of these babies for him!' And then it came over me,—all the love of God for me, and his goodness to me. And when the old woman came back I could ask her to pray with me, and join in the prayer with all my heart."

"And was that the end of your trouble?" asked Veronica.

"Of all the worst of it," said Daisy. "I used to have dark days, and I gave way to temper and to vain repinings; but I could always come back. And then He was so good to me! It seemed, if I may say so, as if He were glad to see me."

"You may say so, I am sure," said Veronica. "There is joy in the presence of the angels of God over one sinner that repenteth."

She took from her pocket a tiny book, and read,—

"This is a sovereign friendship of our gracious Lord, that He keepeth us so tenderly while we are in our sin; and, furthermore, that He then toucheth us and showeth us our sin by the sweet light of mercy and grace. Then we are stirred of the Holy Ghost unto prayer and desire after Him; and then our Lord showeth Himself to the soul in friendly welcoming, as if it had been in pain and prison, saying, 'My dear son, I am glad thou art come to me in all thy woe! I have all the time been with thee, and now thou findest me still loving thee.'"

"That is it exactly," said Daisy. "He seemed to bring me near Him so gently. I was a great deal better off after I left Adela's house. Mr. Fowler found me a nice, quiet boarding-place, with a good old woman, who was kind to me and the children. I had some vexations with my pupils, to be sure, and some trouble with the singers in the choir; but I escaped the daily and hourly annoyances and the constant trials of temper which made me so unhappy when I was with Adela. I cannot say I was very happy; but I was contented and quiet. Even when my health failed, I could not be miserable, for it seemed as though God would take care of me and my children. And so He has. I am happy now,—very happy."

Daisy continued in the same frame as long as she lived, grateful to every one who was kind to her, patient and smiling to the very last. Anne came often to see her, but never stayed long. She had no control over her feelings, and her tears agitated Daisy and brought on her coughing-fits.

Anne had quite decided that she liked Kitty the best. She had already provided a superb wardrobe for the baby, revelling in worked frocks and petticoats, and the broadest ribbon sashes that could be bought for money. Her nursery was furnished with all the modern improvements, and was proudly displayed to all her acquaintances, many of whom laughed behind her back and wondered how long the new freak would last. Meantime, Veronica worked at her cashmere frocks and bird's-eye aprons, while Becky cooked nice things to tempt Daisy's appetite, and revived her knowledge of ornamental stiches till she made Rosy's new socks into wonders of art. Mark was very busy, but he contrived to steal time from his numerous avocations to see Daisy and the baby, and to carve out of soft pine and cedar some wonderful figures of cows and sheep, and a shepherd and shepherdess, as toys for Rosy. The little lady took to him at once, and won his whole heart from the first time she clawed her little hands into his beard; and he was impatient for the time when he should have her at home.

The time came very soon. Daisy sunk away at the close of a sunny winter's day,—passing away as quietly as the sunset-clouds whose pink reflection shone on her pale face.

"It is all over!" said Mark, brushing the tears from his eyes. "Her God, in whom she trusted, has delivered her from this present evil world. May He give us grace to guide this child to her mother's arms! I suppose it will be best to take the children away pretty soon?"

"Perhaps it will be as well," replied the Sister who had charge of the twins. "The longer I keep them, the harder it will be to part with them."

Mr. John Campion provided for the expenses of the simple funeral, and Daisy was laid to rest by the side of Veronica's own babies, under the forest-trees of Mount Faith, there to await her joyous resurrection; and the same day the children were removed to their new homes.

Becky was at the door, eagerly watching for the carriage, and stretched out her arms for the baby.

"Fast asleep," said Veronica, as Mark handed her out. "Carry her in, Becky, and lay her on the bed. I dare say she will be lonely just at first; but she will soon be reconciled to the change. Children at that age have short memories."

"Dear lamb!" said Becky, carefully laying down her precious charge. "How nice it seems to have a baby in my arms once more! I wish we could have had them both."

"That was quite out of the question," replied Veronica. "To say nothing of any other consideration, it would not have been fair to

Mrs. John to deprive her of the child after she had set her heart upon it."

"No," said Becky, reflectively: "I suppose not. She has provided beautiful clothes for the child, I must say. They quite take the shine off ours. Such lovely sashes and **frocks!** I can't help wishing Rosy could have some like them."

"You must not think of such a thing," said Veronica. "We cannot pretend to compete with Mrs. John in such matters; and whatever money we have to spend for Rosy must be saved for a time when she will need it more than now."

"Well, I suppose that is so," said Becky, in whose mind always rankled a certain bitterness that Mr. John Campion should have become so much richer than her favourite Mr. Mark. "And, anyhow, I cannot see the sense of dressing children in white frocks in cold weather, if one had ever so much money."

"Nor I," replied Veronica. "I can see no beauty in a custom which seems so very inappropriate to the climate; and the danger from fire is something not to be thought of without a shudder."

Rosy slept till after dinner, and awoke

smiling and happy to her supper of bread and milk. She was soon seated on the carpet, surrounded by her stock of new playthings, and taking up one after another with a quiet, observant curiosity which diverted Mark greatly.

"The child will have a turn for science," said he, laughing. "She accepts nothing without investigation."

"I see you are planning her future already," said Veronica.

"Why, my dear, you know it is my nature to look forward. I am always at least three chapters ahead in my book."

"I foresee that the said book is provided with a formidable rival," remarked Veronica. "You must not let the new child interfere with the claims of the old one. You ought to be well forward with it; and you have lost a good deal of time during the last two weeks."

"Oh, Veronica, what a merciless taskmaster you are!" groaned Mark, looking at his desk. "Do let me have this one evening to play with baby."

"Oh, you need not put on that injured air, —as Anne says when I object to her contradicting my orders," said Veronica, gayly. "I had no intention of setting you to work to-night."

"But I must go to work of my own accord, though," said Mark, starting up. "I promised Bacon to come down and correct those **proofs** this very night. We will have prayer before I go. Don't sit up for me, Veronica. **I shall** be sure to be late."

"There is one thing that puzzles me," said Becky, thoughtfully. Rosy was in bed by this time, and Becky had brought her knitting to the parlour fireside. She **often** did so when Veronica was alone,—thus affording another ground of stricture to Anne, who "wondered" that Veronica could allow Becky to take such liberties. Becky was sitting bolt upright, according to custom, in the hard, straight-backed chair which she affected on these occasions, her **knitting-work** progressing with the regularity of machinery.

"There is one thing which always puzzles me," she replied, laying down her knitting, and thoughtfully scratching her head with the needle.

"**If** there is only one **thing**, Becky, you are better off than most of us," replied Veronica, rousing herself from a fit of abstraction. "But what is your particular puzzle just now?"

"Well, it is none of my business, exactly,"

said Becky, in rather an apologetic tone. "I was wondering how it happens that Mr. John should have been so much more successful than Mr. Mark. Mr. Mark has more sense in his little finger than Mr. John has in his whole body. Yes, he has, Mrs. Mark," she repeated, anticipating an interruption from Veronica. "I was brought up with them, and I ought to know; and every one liked Mr. Mark the best. I don't see how it is."

"Are you quite sure it is so, Becky?" asked Veronica. "Are you quite certain that Mr. John is the most successful?"

"Well, he is the richest, if you come to that," said Becky.

"There can be no question of that; but making money is only one kind of success,— nay, it may be, no success at all."

Becky looked doubtful.

Veronica proceeded:—"A successful man is a man who attains the object upon which he has set his heart; and unless one knows what that object is, one cannot tell whether he is successful or not."

"Mr. John set his heart upon getting rich from the time he was a little boy," observed Becky. "I have often heard him talk about it. He always said he would make a fortune and then sit down and enjoy it."

"Exactly; and how much is a fortune?"

"A fortune is generally a little more money than folks have got, I think," said Becky.

Veronica laughed. "Exactly so, Becky. That seems to be what Mr. John thinks. He has made money hand over hand for the last ten years. I suppose he is one of the richest men in the city; but he does not seem to have come to the stopping-place, for he works quite as hard and allows himself just as little recreation as he did when he first began business. So it seems he cannot be called a successful man, after all."

"Well, now, supposing that is so," said Becky, who was usually very cautious in giving her assent to any thing: "what aim did Mr. Mark set before himself?"

"To glorify God and enjoy him forever," said Veronica, with emphasis. "That was the aim that Mark set before himself early in life; and in that he has certainly succeeded, thus far."

"No one knows that better than I do," returned Becky, with equal emphasis. "If any one ever did glorify God in his life and conversation, that man is Mark Campion. Even in the darkest days, when you were sick, and we were in debt and hardly knew where to turn for the next day's meals, and the dear little boy was taken away, I never heard a murmur or complaint from his lips,—no, not when he had to work half the night to earn the wood which he cut up with his own hands. I have often wondered why so much trouble was allowed to come upon you, of all people in the world. You seemed to need it so little."

"The only answer to all such questions is that of our Father himself:—'As many as I love I rebuke and chasten;' 'All things work together for good to them that love God.' Those are the answers we must rest upon, Becky. I confess with shame that I could not always do so; but I believe Mark's faith never failed for an instant."

"Mine did, I know," said Becky. "But, after all, Mrs. Mark, I cannot help wishing sometimes that Mr. Mark was rich, so that he need not have to work so hard."

"Hard work is good for him, Becky. Don't you know that his spirits and health are always best when he has the most upon his hands? I do wish sometimes, however, that he was not obliged to work so late at night. It is bad for his eyes. But I think we are pretty well off at present, Becky: don't you? What do we want very much that we do not have?"

"Well, I don't know," said Becky, considering. "I should like you to have a carriage and horses: only then we should have to keep a man, and that is such a bother."

Becky always spoke of men in the abstract as though they were noxious animals, not to be endured about the house except in cases of the utmost need.

"We have always the street-cars, you know," said Veronica. "Well, what next?"

"Well, let me see. There would be no use in furnishing this room any smarter, as long as we use it so commonly; and I can't see the use of rooms if you don't use them. I am sure this old ingrain carpet is easier to sweep than a Brussels or velvet,—especially as Mr. Mark will scatter his shavings from one end of it to the other. Besides, this room, just as it is, looks prettier than Mrs. John's grand parlours, after all. Somehow, her rooms never have a home-like look. I don't think any rooms ever look so, where people never have any thing doing."

"I agree with you there, Becky. No room seems pleasant to me where there are no workbaskets, or ink-stands, or books made to be read, or newspapers, or magazines. But, I confess, I should like to have money enough to fit up the side room properly with bookcases and make a library of it."

"You would hardly want to do that just now." observed Becky, folding up her knitting. "A bedroom down-stairs is a great convenience when there is a baby about. Well, Mrs. Mark, I guess I'll go to bed. You ought to go too; but of course you won't: so there is no use in talking. I'll just make up the cakes, and take one look at the baby. Bless her little heart! she is sleeping just like a picture."

CHAPTER IV.

MISS BROWN.

A FEW days after the coming of the babies, Veronica called upon her sister-in-law. She found her seated in her new nursery, holding the little Kitty, and amusing her with a "crying baby," while various other expensive toys were scattered about the floor. Kitty was splendidly dressed in white, with a Roman scarf a quarter of a yard wide for a sash. The room was warm; but the child's bare arms looked red and mottled. Anne held her up for Aunt Veronica's inspection, with a not unjustifiable pride; and certainly the little creature did look very pretty indeed.

"Now, is not that a handsome frock?" said Anne. "Did you ever see such open-work in your life? It is more like lace than cambric."

"It is certainly very beautiful," said Veronica. "Who did it? Mrs. Wicks, I suppose?"

"No, indeed," replied Anne, colouring. "Mrs. Wicks will never do a stitch of work for me again. Just think! she had the impudence to send her bill to John, because she said I kept her waiting so long for those worked petticoats. And it was only forgetfulness on my part, too; for I had the money by me all the time. John came home and scolded me like every thing about it. He said he never interfered with my finery, but he would not allow me to make debts. 'Well,' said I, 'Mrs. Wicks has got her money, but she has lost a customer. I will never go to her again.' And I never have. Miss White worked all Kitty's things."

"Mrs. Wicks is very poor, you know, Anne, and she has had a great deal of expense with her family: so she may perhaps be excused for a little over-eagerness. She told me herself she was sorry for what she had done, but she did not know which way to turn for money."

"I can't help it," persisted Anne. "If anybody affronts me once, they don't have a chance to do so again. I allow of no interference in my concerns."

Veronica could not forbear smiling, but she made no remark, and only said, "Miss White certainly works very nicely. But are you not afraid of Kitty's taking cold, with these bare arms? You know she is transplanted from a warm climate."

"Oh, well, I don't believe in coddling children," replied Anne. "I believe they may as well be hardy as tender, if people only think so. I always thought you kept yours too warm; and that was one thing which ailed them. There, now! don't put on your martyr face. I don't mean to hurt your feelings: only you are so wonderfully sensitive and touchy."

"I think nature herself teaches us that young creatures are to be kept warm," said Veronica, who knew by experience that the only way to defend herself from Anne's accusations was to disregard them. "See how much pains she takes with young birds, how the cat cuddles her little kittens, and the dog her puppies, and even how the buds upon the trees are wrapped up. Dr. Warren says that Boston sacrifices about five hundred babies a year to the fashion of short sleeves and bare necks."

"Dr. Warren is an old fogy," said Anne,

peevishly. "Do you suppose if short sleeves had been **so bad for** babies, people would not have found it out by this time? I do hate to see the little things fussed up with long sleeves, like old women. Oh, Kitty, what have you done? You have pulled poor baby's head off! Now it cannot cry any more. But never mind, darling: mamma will buy you another. **If you** want to buy one for Rosy, Veronica, **they** have them at Smith's."

"Rosy will have to play with dolls of home manufacture, at present," said Veronica. "I have made her one with which she is perfectly satisfied, and which has the advantage of not being breakable. I think such pretty and expensive toys are thrown away upon little children. They are soon soiled and broken and lose their novelty, and by the time the children are old enough to appreciate them **they have** become **an** old story. I wish to keep Rosy contented with cheap and small pleasures as long as possible."

"Well, I suppose it **is** only prudent in her case, as the poor child has so little to look forward to," said Anne. "But I must tell you, Veronica, that it will not do to make such a very marked difference between the children in point of dress. People will remark upon it if you do so."

"If people will not mind their own business, it is no fault of mine," said Veronica, not without emphasis. "I shall dress Rosy according to my means and the best of my judgment; and I certainly shall not expend upon finery for a baby the money which will be needed for her education by-and-by."

"If you had not been willing to take some trouble and make some sacrifices for the child, you ought not to have taken her," said Anne. "I shall talk to Mark about it."

"Do; and I will talk to John about Kitty's short sleeves and the danger of her setting herself on fire with her muslin frocks," said Veronica, laughing. "Which of us do you think would stand the best chance of being heard? Seriously, Anne, I must act according to the best of my judgment about this child. I have taken her for my own, and I must rear her as my own. I cannot be dictated to by anybody."

"Who wants to dictate?" said Anne, peevishly. "You think yourself so very perfect, that if any one gives you the least hint, or intimates that you may be to blame in any thing, you fly into a passion. I think it's very hard, after all I have done for you, if I cannot give you a little advice. But I don't expect any gratitude for what I do for people. I have given all that up long ago."

"As to that," said Veronica, "if we were to reckon up the items, we should perhaps find the account more nearly balanced than you think. Moreover, you should remember that benefits with which one is constantly reproached cease to be benefits, and become injuries. But come, Anne; do not let us quarrel. You will take your course, and I must take mine; but we need not interfere with one another. These dear babies ought to be a bond of union, instead of a cause of discord."

"I am sure I don't want to quarrel; only you are so touchy," said Anne.

"Well, let bygones be bygones," returned Veronica. "Can you give me a pattern for a baby's cloak? Mrs. Kirkland has none that I think pretty."

In displaying and commenting on Kitty's various outer garments, all Anne's ill humour vanished,—as, to do her justice, it was apt to do after a short indulgence,—and the sisters-in-law parted excellent friends.

"Becky," said Veronica, one day, after dinner, "have you heard any thing about Miss Brown lately? I have been so busy with the baby, and all the rest, that I have hardly thought of her. I believe I will carry her some of this apple-pudding. It will be just the thing she will be likely to fancy."

"I will carry it to her myself," replied Becky. "You have been out once, and that is enough. Poor thing! if one could do any thing to comfort her, one ought to be willing, I am sure."

Becky was soon on her way, with her basin, and some of her famous light cakes, wrapped in a white napkin. She was met at the door of Miss Brown's house by a young, crabbed-looking woman, with a whining child in her arms. She seemed annoyed by Becky's inquiry for her aunt, and answered, rather unwillingly,—

"She is pretty comfortable, I believe: at least, I have not seen her for some days."

"Not seen her!" exclaimed Becky. "What do you mean by that?"

"Why, you see, Rebecca, aunt was not very comfortable here,—at least, she was not at all contented,—and the house is so small and inconvenient, and we thought she would perhaps be happier with some one else; and so——"

"Out with it!" said Rebecca, bluntly. "Have you sent her to the poor-house? It is no more than I have been expecting."

"No," returned Martha. "The poor-house, indeed! But she has gone to the Old Ladies' Home; and I only hope she will like the change as much as we do."

"To the Old—Ladies'—Home!" repeated Rebecca, slowly. "And so, Martha, after all the rest, you have finished up by turning the poor old woman out of her own house to die among strangers!"

"I'm sure we had hard work enough to raise the money," said Martha, beginning to whimper. "We had to pay two hundred dollars down, for all it is called a charitable institution; and we have always paid the taxes upon the house, ever since we came to live here: so it ought to be ours, I am sure."

"Yes,—out of your aunt's money, that she put into your hands, like an old fool as she was!" interrupted Becky.

"And aunt has a parlour and bedroom of her own, and closet beside,—which is more than she needs, in my opinion," continued Martha, in the same tone. "We have had to let her take furniture for them; and now she wants the secretary and sofa, and I don't see how we can spare them. I wish people would just let us alone!"

"Oh, we shall let you alone, never fear," said Rebecca, grimly. "You don't suppose any of us are coming here for *your* sake, do you? Only just let me tell you, at parting, if the judgment of Heaven don't fall on you in some shape, Martha Brown, I shall be mistaken. Your days will not be long in the land, I guess. I wonder you dare look at that child in your arms, when you think how you have treated the woman who was a mother to you when your own mother abandoned you in her shame. Oh, yes! you see I know all about it; and so shall other folks, I promise you, unless you do the poor old woman justice. Every one round here thinks you are Miss Brown's niece; but I know better. I well remember your mother,—poor wretch!—and how she died, too."

"I'm sure, Rebecca, you won't be so cruel as to bring up all that story?" whimpered Martha. "Even Tom's family don't know any thing about it."

"Let me see how you behave, and then I will tell you what I will do," replied Becky, turning away.

"You may as well leave what you have got in your basin," said Martha. "You won't want to carry it back again."

"Oh, it a'n't heavy," returned Becky. "I would not presume to offer it to folks that have got a house of their own. Good-by, Martha. I hope your sin won't be visited on your children: that's all!"

"Why have you brought your pudding back again?" said Veronica, in surprise. "What has happened?"

"The old lady has moved," replied Becky.

"What do you mean?"

"Or, rather, she has been moved," continued Becky. "They have sent her to the Old Ladies' Home. I gave Martha a piece of my mind at parting: that is one comfort. She wanted me to leave the pudding for her; but I wasn't going to do that, anyhow."

"And so they have sent the poor woman away from her own home, to finish her days in an almshouse!" said Veronica. "Not but she will be a hundred times better off in the Home;—but what black ingratitude! I wonder if Martha can know any thing of her own true history."

"Oh, yes: she knows it, and, more than that, she knows that I know it, too," said Becky. "I told her as much to-day. Folks say adopted children almost always turn out that way. I hope this darling won't."

"I trust not, Becky. At any rate, we will not borrow any trouble about it yet. I will try to go round and see Miss Brown to-morrow. She must think it strange that I have not been near her."

The next day Veronica put Rosy in her little carriage, one of the few new things which had been bought for her, and went to pay a visit to Miss Brown. The Old Ladies' Home was a charitable institution, richly endowed by two old maiden ladies, both with lands and money, for the benefit of sixteen single women and widows of good report, who should bring their own beds and tables and two hundred dollars in money. The bequest had greatly increased in value during forty years, and, as the funds were honestly managed and none of them diverted for any other purpose, the old ladies were made extremely comfortable. Veronica found Miss Brown in a good-sized and lofty room, well furnished with carpet and curtains, a pleasant, sunshiny window, and a nice little stove at which she could prepare her own meals, if she preferred doing so to going to the public table. A door near the fireplace opened into a small but very neat bedroom, and another, with glass in the top, into a large pantry or storeroom. The sun shone in pleasantly, the room looked cheerful and orderly, and as Veronica entered and glanced about her she thought her old friend had decidedly changed for the better.

"It is very good in you to come and find me out so soon," said Miss Brown, rising from her arm-chair to greet her friend. "I have been looking for you, and should have sent you word of the change I have made; but I had no messenger. And who is this little girl?"

"This is my little daughter Rosy," replied Veronica. "She and her concerns have been the cause of my long absence: so I thought I would bring her to make her own apology. We have adopted her in the place of those God has taken to Himself."

"Pretty darling!" said Miss Brown, with tears in her eyes. "I hope she may be a comfort to you, Veronica. Is she an orphan?"

"Yes. Her father died before she was born, and her mother, an old schoolmate of mine, was buried two or three weeks ago. She has a twin sister, whom Mrs. John Campion has taken for her own."

"And have the children no family friends at all?"

"No one but an aunt, who lives in New Orleans and is not likely to interfere with them."

"So much the better for you," said Miss Brown. "I hope God will give you grace to train this child up in the way she should go, and make her a blessing to you. What shall I find to amuse her?"

"She will be very well contented with any thing or nothing," said Veronica. "That basket of yarn balls will be a great delight, if there is nothing in it which she can hurt. She seems to have a faculty of amusing herself, and will sit on the floor for two hours at a time, as happy as a kitten."

"That is an excellent habit, and one to be cultivated by all means," said Miss Brown. "Veronica, whatever you do, don't make yourself a slave to the child. Make her understand early that it is her place to please and wait upon you. You will both be the happier for it in the end."

"I believe you are right," said Veronica, thoughtfully. "It is more blessed to give than to receive."

"That was the mistake I made from the first," continued Miss Brown, resuming her knitting. "I made myself a slave to Martha. I humoured her in every fancy. No matter what I was doing, I laid aside every thing to amuse and gratify her. Ah, it was a great mistake!"

"It does not excuse Martha, however," said Veronica.

"I made another great mistake in my anxiety to secure the child's affection," continued Miss Brown. "I never governed her. I thought she would not love me if I contradicted her, and so I let her have her own way in every thing. I did not teach her to fear God,—for I hardly knew Him myself in those days,—and I did not teach her to treat me with even common respect. I well remember one day, when Martha was about four years old, a neighbour came in, and I was telling her of something the child had done. 'I didn't, either, any such thing,' said Martha, in her lisping way. 'Don't be so ridiculous, aunty!' I laughed, and thought it very smart; but the neighbour looked grave. 'That sounds amusing now,' said she; 'but how will it sound when she is twelve or fourteen?' '**Oh, she will know** better by that time,' said I. But when I tried to teach her better I found it was not so easy. I had trained her to think all I did for her no more than her due. If I did not work for her, I was greatly to blame. If **I** did, it was no more than she had a right to expect; and she never dreamed of thanking me. Ah, it was a great mistake! I ruined the child I wished to benefit, and prepared a bed of thorns for my old age. **May** God forgive me!"

"You must not reproach yourself too deeply," said Veronica, kindly. "You acted for the best."

"No," replied Miss Brown, shaking her head: "I dare not think so. It was selfishness, Veronica,—selfish love of ease and fear of trouble. It distressed me to hear the child cry and to see that she was unhappy. She had a strong will,—at least, she was very wilful,—and it seemed so much easier at the time to let her have her own way, or to coax her into doing what I wanted, than it was to contradict her. I hope God will forgive me,—nay, I believe He *has* forgiven me; but I must bear the sting of seeing the fruit of my doings constantly before my eyes. I pray night and day that it may not be visited on Martha and her children."

"Was not your move rather a sudden one?" asked Veronica, willing to divert her old friend from such a painful topic. "I heard nothing of it till Becky went over to see you last night."

"Very sudden to me," said Miss Brown; "though I believe Martha and her husband have had it in contemplation for a long time, and were only waiting for me to reach the required age. I was sixty years old only a day or two before Martha came into my room and told me that Thomas had paid the money into the Home for me, and that my room was ready. It gave me a terrible shock, I must confess, and at first I almost thought I could not bear the change; but I soon found I could not help myself. I had put the house out of my hands with my other property, and I had made no stipulation as to a home for myself. But the furniture in the house is still mine; and I should like to have a little more of it, particularly my dear mother's sofa, and the secretary, arm-chair, and clock which belonged to my father's study. I have his books, as you see," (pointing to a glass corner-cupboard containing a large number of well-bound and carefully-preserved volumes.) "I believe Martha thought them only so much useless lumber, and not worth house-room. But I should like to have the other things, if possible."

"I will see what can be done," said Veronica, who thought she saw her way to a solution of the difficulty. "Do you find yourself comfortable here?"

"Very much so. They are all kind to me, and I am most bountifully supplied with fuel and provisions. I prepare my own breakfast and tea, as I can thus take my own time about it; and every thing is very handy for me, as you see."

"I must bring you some pictures for your walls," said Veronica. "Mark has heaps of prints and photographs for which we have no room; and you should have some plants in that sunny window."

"I should like them very much, and also

a little dog or cat to keep me company. I miss the children."

"I think I can help you to one," said Veronica. "My sister-in-law has a very pretty little black spaniel for which she wishes to find a home, and I am sure she would be pleased to give it to you. I will see her about it to-day."

Veronica only stopped at home long enough to give Rosy into Rebecca's charge, and then went straight down to her brother-in-law's office. She was fortunate enough to find him alone. John waked up from his abstraction at the sight of Veronica, for whom he had a great regard and respect, and listened to her story with great attention.

"I do not know that you can do any thing about it, brother," she concluded, "but I know you have business dealings with Thomas James, and——"

"Yes, yes," said John, rubbing his eye-glasses. "I will attend to the matter. I told the old lady she was foolish to trust him so far; but of course she wouldn't be advised. How is the baby? The most wonderful child that ever lived, of course."

"We think so," said Veronica, smiling.

"And so do we. I want to make Rosy a present, Veronica," John continued, putting his hand into his pocket and drawing out a gold piece; "but I never know what to buy for children: so I leave it to you. As for Miss Brown, the old lady shall have her furniture. I know where to put the screws on."

How the screws were to be put on, Veronica did not inquire, and, to say the truth, did not greatly care. She knew that her brother-in-law was a just and prudent man, and not one to let the grass grow under his feet. She called on Anne and secured the spaniel for Miss Brown, and then went home, well satisfied with her morning's work. A few days afterwards, going to carry the dog to its new home, she found Miss Brown rejoicing in the possession of her household goods, with the tall clock ticking away in the corner, and the little bird in the top, popping out of his house to proclaim the hours, as though he had never lived anywhere else. The screws had evidently been applied to good purpose.

CHAPTER IV.

MISUNDERSTANDING.

"COME to tea, Veronica, you and Mark, and bring Rosy with you. I want to see the children together. You have not been at our house to tea this winter. Now, promise you will come."

"I cannot promise for Mark till I have seen him; but you may expect Rosy and Rosy's mamma," said Veronica. "I am going down town, and will speak to Mark on my way; and I promise you, if it be possible, I will bring him out to-night."

"Mark is very unsocial," said Anne. "It seems the hardest work in the world to drag him out anywhere."

"I admit that he is apt to be remiss in his social duties," replied Veronica, smiling. "His dressing-gown and his whittling, as Becky disrespectfully calls his wood-carving, have such charms for him, after a hard day's work, that it is very difficult to induce him to leave them for the 'customary suit of solemn black' required on social occasions. But, if you will allow him to come in his gray clothes, I will see what I can do."

This conversation passed between the sisters-in-law, in Anne Campion's drawing-room, about four months after the adoption of the children. In spite of Becky's prophecy, Anne had not "grown tired of her doll." On the contrary, she seemed to become more and more fond of it every day. Kitty was a wonderfully engaging child, and soon wound herself very closely round the hearts of the household, —even of John Campion, who had never before been known to take the slightest notice of any baby.

Child-like, Kitty soon found out her own powers. She discovered that her mamma could not bear to hear her cry, and that to scream for any thing was to get it, if she only screamed loud and long enough. She was not backward in exercising this power. That very morning, Veronica had seen a fine specimen. Kitty caught sight of a very small and very precious pair of china vases mounted in gilt filigree, and, in her pretty, peremptory way, demanded one of them for a plaything.

"Oh, no," said Anne, coaxingly: "**Kitty** cannot have the vase. Kitty would break mamma's pretty vase. Kitty may **have** her blocks with the pictures. See **the** pretty mooly cow." But Kitty had seen the **pretty** mooly cow a great many times, and the vase was a novelty.

"Cup, Kitty! cup!" she repeated, still stretching out her hand.

"How plainly she begins to speak!—doesn't she?" said the fond mother. "No, no. Kitty can have her **own** pretty silver cup, but not mamma's vase."

But Kitty persisted, and at last flung herself on the floor and screamed with all her might.

"There, there! don't cry: mamma's pet shall have the cup; but she must be very careful. She has such a strong will," she added, speaking to Veronica. "It is very hard for her to give up any thing upon which she sets **her heart.** I think she will have a great deal of force of character and perseverance in whatever she undertakes."

"Perhaps so," replied Veronica; "but I

don't think that perseverance and wilfulness always go together: do you?"

"I suppose you would not have given her the vase if she had screamed herself into convulsions," said Anne; "but my notions are different. I like to see character **develop** itself freely and in its own way. It **makes** children artificial and deceitful to put such a restraint upon them as many people do. Besides, I think it very bad for children to cry. I am convinced that it affects their heads."

Veronica made no answer to this oracular theory, but she could not help thinking that it depended upon the kind of character whether it should be allowed to develop itself freely or not. She saw that Anne was laying up trouble both for herself and the child; but she knew by experience that it was worse than useless for her to say any thing.

Creeping to the other end of the room, Kitty turned her new plaything over a few times, and then, taking it by the handle, she began pounding it with all her small force upon the floor. Anne sprang to the rescue; but she was too late. The precious pale-green china flew into fragments, which were scattered far and wide.

"You naughty, naughty child!" exclaimed

Anne. "You have ruined mamma's pretty vase, that she gave five dollars for only yesterday. Naughty Kitty! Mamma does not love her when she does so."

Kitty screamed louder than ever.

"Oh, you are quite intolerable this morning. I shall send for Jane," said Anne, ringing the bell. "Here, Jane, take Miss Kitty away, and pacify her, if you can. My poor little **vase**! Dear me! I think children are troublesome comforts, after all."

"I could have told you that," remarked Veronica. "The best of children make a great deal of trouble; and Kitty and Rosy are just at the trying age."

"It is an interesting age, too, I think," said Anne.

"All ages are interesting to one who really cares for children. But I am sorry for your vase."

"Yes; it spoils the pair, and they are very uncommon," said Anne. "However, children will be children."

"One would not have them any thing else," said Veronica,—thinking, however, that there was a difference in children.

"Kitty is growing a regular little Tartar,"

said Mark, when Veronica repeated Anne's message to him. "I must say, I don't care to have Rosy see a great deal of her."

"We cannot help it, my dear Mark. They must be together more or less, and all we can do is to make the best of matters. There is no need of Kitty being a Tartar, any more than Rosy; but when she finds out that she has only to cry for a valuable piece of china to have it given her for a plaything, it is no wonder that she cries. You would soon find Rosy doing the same thing, under the same circumstances."

"It is a great pity, for the sake of the child, if for nothing else," said Mark, thoughtfully. "Cannot you give her a hint, Veronica? You have had so much more experience with children than she has, you know."

"The idea of Anne's taking a hint from me about any thing!" said Veronica, laughing. "Besides, she acts according to her theory of education. She says that character should be allowed to develop itself freely."

"Oh, if she has a theory of education, I have done," replied Mark. "There is no more to be said: only, I am sorry for the child. But cannot you let me off for to-night, Veronica?

You and Rosy can go, and I will come for you."

"I neither can nor will let you off," said Veronica. "You are to bear your share of the duties of life, as well as other people; and it is not kind to Anne to refuse her express invitation for no better reason than because you are lazy. I will tell you, for your comfort, however, that Anne says you may come in your gray clothes. Now, mind you don't disappoint me."

Mark gave a grunt of resignation and acquiescence, and returned to his writing. He would have pleaded fatigue and stupidity when tea-time came, but Veronica was inexorable, and produced him in Anne's parlour at the time appointed. She had expended part of Uncle John's gold piece on a delicate rose-coloured merino frock for baby, which she had pleased herself with embroidering to the extent of her skill.

"Well, Veronica, I must say, you do make the child look very pretty,—very, indeed," said Anne, as the little girl's wrappings were removed. "If it were not for those odious long sleeves, I don't know but I should like the coloured frocks as well as white ones; and they certainly do save a great deal of trouble; but the sleeves spoil every thing. Let me take off her sack for once:—there! see how much prettier she looks. Come, now, do have them off."

"When summer comes," said Veronica, smiling. "I should not dare to take them off now."

"Well, I must say, you are very obstinate. Just see how well Kitty has been all winter."

"Kitty is stronger than Rosy; and, moreover, I think I have heard of Kitty's having more than two or three bad colds. But, Anne, just make the case your own. How would you like to go about the house these cold days with your neck and arms all bare?"

"It is different with children," said Anne.

"I do not know why. However, there is no particular use in arguing the case any more, that I know of. Please to admire my wreath of oak-leaves and acorns. It is my own design and my own work."

"It is lovely," said Anne. "I always say you have the prettiest patterns of any one. I wish you would make one for me."

"I will make any number of patterns for you," replied Veronica; "but I rather doubt

Miss White's willingness to work after my designs. She has a great conceit of her talent in that way. Now let us go down-stairs, or Mark will think himself deserted, and run away home."

"So you really did come, Mark? It is more than I expected," said Anne. "You shall have a grand cup of coffee to pay for your extra goodness."

"Thank you. You know I appreciate your coffee, Anne. Veronica never will let me have it strong enough. She pretends it is all for my good, you know," he added, confidentially; "but I know better. It is because Becky is stingy, and Veronica dares not contradict her. Halloo, Kittens! Come and see Uncle Mark. Up she goes! That's the way to play with kittens."

"Take care," said Veronica. "Kitty is not used to such rough play. She has no one to make a ball of her, as you do of Rosy."

"Oh, yes! John romps with her half the evening. I often think he will break her neck. But, Mark, now don't you think that babies look prettier in low necks and short sleeves? Don't you think Rosy would look better if she were dressed like Kitty, instead of being fussed up like an old woman, as she is now?"

This was one of Anne's "ways." She never knew how to let drop a disputed point, be it ever so small, but would bring it up again and again, and upon all occasions.

"I never saw an old woman in a short red frock and white apron," said Mark, gravely. "As to the short sleeves, I certainly agree with you that they are very pretty."

"There, Veronica!" exclaimed Anne: "I knew Mark would say so. Any one with any taste would agree with me."

"I generally think children look all the prettier the less clothes they have on," continued Mark, seriously. "I once saw half a dozen little New Zealand girls elegantly dressed in one large blue bead apiece; and I never saw children look prettier. Nevertheless, I think such a costume would look rather too cool and airy in this climate; and I think the same objection applies to short sleeves in winter."

"Nonsense, Mark! That is very different."

"A difference in degree, but not in kind, my dear sister,—though I admit the degree is a long one."

"There is no use in talking to men about

such things," said Anne. "They never can understand."

"I am fully conscious of my deficiencies in that respect," said Mark, meekly; "and therefore I leave all such subjects to my wife. I never have an opinion of my own after I have passed the door of my own house. I put all my self-appreciation in my pocket with my latch-key at night, and never take it out till I reach the office next morning. I used to have some spirit before I was married, I believe; but Veronica and Becky, between them, have taken it all out of me."

"Becky, indeed! I would soon teach Becky her place," said Anne, with dignity. "She would never go on so in my house, I promise you."

"She would not go on at all in your house; because you would not live together a week," said Veronica. "Becky has her faults, I admit, and sometimes she is disposed to be rather tyrannical; but we have learned to know each other's ways, and we have rubbed through too many hard times together to part easily. Her great fault is an unwillingness to allow the family quite enough to eat."

"I am not sure but that is a good fault,

after all," said Anne. "Our new cook makes away with groceries at a dreadful rate. She actually used up fifteen pounds of butter in one week, Veronica! What do you think of that?"

"I think she never used it at all," replied Veronica.

"Sometimes I think so too," said Anne. "And yet I do not like to believe that such a nice, pleasant-mannered woman would rob me. She has lived in the best families, too."

"So she says."

"Why, don't you believe it?"

"I neither believe nor disbelieve it, Anne. I know nothing about the matter; but what is that to the purpose, if the woman is wasteful or dishonest?"

Anne did not know, exactly, and therefore turned the conversation.

"Please to admire your present, Uncle John," said Veronica, directing his attention to Rosy's frock.

"My present?" said John, who had forgotten all about the matter. "Well, I am sure the child looks very neat and comfortable,—very creditable to you, Veronica, I must say. Anne, why don't you put such frocks and aprons on

Kitty? Her arms are always cold. Just feel them now,—even in this warm room."

Here was an unexpected blow. John hardly ever noticed any article of dress. Anne coloured, and darted an angry glance at Veronica, as though suspecting her of prompting the question, as she answered, sharply, "I suppose I can dress my own child as I please."

"That depends," said John. "Why, the child has got on muslin frocks, as I am alive!" he exclaimed, just awakened to the fact, though the said frocks had been before his eyes all winter. "Muslin frocks, with the thermometer almost at zero! Who ever heard of such a thing? Put a woollen frock on her, directly."

"She has not a woollen frock in the world," said Anne. "Nobody of any taste—no one who can afford to dress children decently—puts coloured frocks upon babies before they are three years old."

"Veronica does, you see."

"Veronica may do as she pleases, and I shall do as I please," said Anne.

"Mrs. Campion," said John, deliberately, "you will have some woollen frocks with long sleeves made for that child, and keep them on her till the weather is warm,—*warm*, do you hear? Let them be bought and made to-morrow; and there is the money to pay for them." And he tossed some bills across the table to his wife. "It is no wonder the child is threatened with croup every other week. I wonder how she has lived at all, such a winter as we have had."

John very rarely took these fits of authority; but, when he did, he regarded neither time nor place, and his decrees were as absolute as those of the Medes and Persians. This Anne knew very well, and she also knew that there was no use in venting any irritation on her husband, as he minded her no more than the rhinoceros minds the birds pecking on his back. So she turned the vials of her wrath upon Veronica, whom she chose to consider the cause of this outbreak.

"Come into my room and have a smoke," said John to his brother, after tea. "I have some prime Turkish tobacco,—real Latakia."

"I have given up smoking for some time," replied Mark. "I found it too expensive a vice for a poor man. However, I don't mind, just for once, if Veronica gives me leave."

"Oh, I dare say Veronica will give you leave, since it is at John's expense," said Anne, unable to repress her vexation any longer. "We have all heard of the man who could drink any *given* quantity." This polite speech was lost upon Mark, who had closed the door behind him, and Anne at once turned the current of her wrath upon Veronica.

"Well, Veronica, I must say, you have played your cards well. John told me one day that you had been at his office; but I really never imagined what your errand was. I will thank you, however, not to interfere between me and my husband again."

"But, Anne, I have not interfered," replied Veronica, gently. "I have not been to the office since Christmas-time; and then I never mentioned Kitty's name. My errand related to some business which I wished to have done for Miss Brown. But, even if I had done so, it would be no worse than your appeal to Mark about Rosy's dress."

"I did that openly," said Anne, a little taken aback. "I did not go to work to undermine you and make mischief behind your back. It is a shame,—so—and about my own child, too!" she added, in tears. "You had better take the baby away at once, if that is the course you mean to take. I am sure I never would have had any thing to do with her, if I had known——" Anne's voice was drowned in sobs.

"Anne, don't be a baby yourself," said Veronica. "Do listen to reason. I have never said one word to John or yourself about the dress or management of Kitty, since you have had her, except when you have asked my opinion. I should not think of such a thing. Neither have I ever interfered with any affair of yours since you were married. You know best whether you can say the same of mine."

"And there are all her nine frocks just good for nothing!" continued Anne. "Such pains as I took with them! and every one said she was the best-dressed child in the street."

"The white frocks will be just as pretty next summer," said Veronica, consolingly; "and you can make the merino frocks as elegantly as you please. I will work you one like Rosy's, if you like. And moreover, Anne, I think white frocks are really going out. I called at Cedar Hill yesterday, and saw Mrs. Miller's children; and they all had coloured frocks,—even the baby. You know she is always in the height of fashion."

"To be sure, I might have white cashmere

for her best; and, I must say, John has been very liberal," said Anne, brightening up a little, and counting her cash. "But, for all that, Veronica, I do think you did wrong to interfere."

"But, Anne, I did not interfere. I never said one word," replied Veronica,—hardly knowing whether to be angry or amused. "Have you ever found me out in a great many lies, that you refuse to believe me now?"

"Oh, well, perhaps you did not mean to; but you certainly did," said Anne. "There are other ways of interfering besides in words. However, I shall say no more: only, this must be the last time. I have borne a great deal from you, but I cannot have you making mischief between me and my husband. That is the one thing I won't stand."

Veronica's patience with Anne was a threefold cord, not easily broken; but perhaps it had been considerably chafed in former encounters, for it now snapped all at once. She rose, and began putting up her work.

"Where are you going?" asked Anne, surprised, as she always was upon such occasions.

"I am going home," said Veronica, distinctly. "When you can learn not to insult your invited guest in your own house, I may perhaps return, and not before. Come, Rosy."

"Why, Veronica, what do you mean? How have I insulted you?"

"By calling me a mischief-maker, and by more than insinuating that I am a liar."

"Why, Veronica, how can you say so? I did not mean any such thing. I only meant——"

"You only meant to vent your ill humour on the person you thought would bear it best, I suppose," said Veronica, as Anne paused, not quite knowing what she intended to say; "but you must understand, Anne, that if we are to be friends you must learn to rein your tongue. I shall not submit to such treatment."

"Oh, don't go, Veronica," exclaimed Anne, really frightened. "John will be so angry."

"That is your affair, not mine."

"And I am sure I did not mean any thing," continued Anne: "only, I was provoked with John for coming out in that way before you, and I did not know what I said. And I have got such a nice supper, too,—just what I know Mark likes best. Please don't go. Come;

you know I always say what comes uppermost."

"You would do well to take care what comes uppermost, in that case,—at least so far as I am concerned," said Veronica, yielding, however, to Anne's entreaties, and resuming her seat; "for I tell you, once for all, I shall not feel obliged to endure any more such language."

Anne would perhaps have continued the subject, for she had an undying affection for the last word, and, if she made any apology whatever, she usually spoiled it as soon as made; but, fortunately, she was called from the room, and when she came back she was furnished with a new subject by the wastefulness of the cook, who had used up all the cream, so that there was none for the apricot tarts.

"So you have given up smoking, Mark?" said John, as he offered pipe and tobacco to his brother. "What induced you to do that? You used to be the greatest old chimney I knew."

"Why, smoking is an expensive vice for a poor man, as I told you," replied Mark, in the process of lighting his pipe. "I don't like any tobacco but the best; and that is costly.

Besides, I was in debt; and I have a theory that people who owe money have no right to luxuries."

"That's a good doctrine, anyhow," said his brother, sinking into his favourite arm-chair and putting up his feet luxuriously. "I wish more people held it. But, bless you, the people who owe the most are those who have the most to spend. Who drives such fine horses and makes such a show as the Blairs? And yet Blair cannot hold a cent of property in his own name, and has not done so these ten years."

"That is not my way," said Mark, assuming an equally free-and-easy position on the other side of the fire. "As long as I was in debt, I felt that I was living upon other people's money."

"Well, there is our church, now," continued John. "We are in debt for the **very** ground the house is built upon; and yet we **have** just bought a grand new organ, and a set of painted windows, and I don't know what besides. What do you say to that?"

"The principle seems to me the same," replied Mark: "only, I think such a course is worse in a church than in a private individual, because the example is more widely spread."

"But you are not in debt now, are you, Mark?"

"No,—thank God!" said Mark, devoutly: "I owe no man any thing."

"Then I think you might indulge now and then."

"Well, perhaps so, John; but, after all, I am just as well without tobacco, and better. The money which I should waste in smoke goes for things which do not perish so quickly in the using. Then, I have a new motive to economy, since we have taken the child to bring up. And, to conclude, Veronica doesn't like the smell."

John gave a kind of grunt, which might mean either dissent or approval. "Do you expect to have any thing to leave the child?" he asked, after another interval of silence.

"I don't know. I mean she shall have a thoroughly good education,—as good as I can give her; and I have already doubled my life-insurance for her benefit."

"Right,—quite right," interrupted John.

"And if this book succeeds, as seems likely, I may have something more."

"I read the chapters published in the —— what's its name?" said John. "I am no great judge; but I thought them very clever. And do you keep your premiums paid up? Excuse me for asking,—it is no business of mine,—but it is important to do so; and if you should be short of ready money at any time, you know I can always accommodate you."

"Thank you, John; but I have done very well hitherto."

"Don't hesitate to ask me, if you want money at any time, Mark. We have taken different paths in life; but that is no reason we should not help one another all we can."

"You are very kind, brother," said Mark, with glistening eyes; for he was easily moved, and any expression of affection was rare with John. "If I should need any thing, I will not hesitate to apply to you; but I am really doing very well. It was only my long illness and poor Becky's mishap, with the sickness and death of our Annie, that threw me back. We are all well now,—thank God! My wife is the best manager in the world, and puts money in my purse instead of taking it out. Our wishes are modest, you know; and really we are very comfortable."

"John," continued Mark, after an interval of some minutes, "will you excuse me if I ask you a question about your own business?"

"Fire away," said John. "What now?"

"Have you ever made a will?"

"Long ago. Just after I was married. You will find I have not forgotten you, old fellow."

"That was not what was in my mind," said Mark.

"You need not tell me that, Mark: I know you better. But what were you thinking of?"

"I was thinking of Kitty," said Mark. "Ought you not to make some provision for her?"

"Well, I don't know. I cannot say I had thought of it," said John, putting down his pipe and looking at his brother. "Perhaps it will be best. To tell the truth, Mark,—though I dare say you will think it all nonsense,—a will is about the last business paper that I want to touch. I made my will once, as I said, just after I was married; and I have never looked at it since."

"You are no more likely to die for making your will."

"Of course I know that. It is merely a fancy of mine. But I think you are right about providing for Kitty. It won't do to leave her altogether dependent upon Anne. She is a good woman, but she sometimes takes freaks, and, like other women, she knows nothing at all of business."

"Why don't you teach her, then? Veronica is as good a man of business as I am,—though I dare say you think that is no great praise," he added, smiling as he saw his brother smile. "But now confess, John, that you underrate me. Did not I always pay my interest at the bank to a day?"

"Always; but then confess, Mark, in your turn, that you are not a money-making man."

"Mine is not a money-making trade. I knew that when I took it up. But, if I were you, I would teach Anne to understand common business."

"I should dearly love to see you do it."

"I would certainly try. What is to become of her if she is left to manage for herself?"

"She won't be left to manage for herself. I have taken care of that. As for Veronica, she is one by herself, and no more a rule for other women than our mother was. As to providing for Kitty, depend upon it, Mark, I will see to the matter; and I thank you for reminding me of it. I will add a codicil to my will."

"A codicil to his will? What should he do that for?" thought Anne, who caught the last words as she came to call the gentlemen to supper. "I wonder what Mark has been at now, talking to John about his will? After all, I believe Veronica did say something to John about Kitty's dress. It would be just like her,—always pretending to act from a sense of duty. I shall always think so."

CHAPTER VI.

THE BREACH WIDENS.

AND Anne always did think so. Weeds often take strong root in very shallow soil; and the roots of Anne's prejudices were anchored in the rock,—the stratum of obstinacy which often underlies a weak character. When she once took a dislike to anybody, from whatever cause, that person could nevermore do any thing right in her eyes. Every action, however praiseworthy or however harmless, was distorted to suit her preconceived theory. Under all her consciousness of superiority to Veronica there lurked always an uneasy feeling of jealousy, which was not lessened by John's praises of his sister-in-law, whom he was wont to designate as a "brick," "a regular sensible woman."

This jealousy was nothing new. It dated

back to their school-days, when it was accounted a great triumph to put Saint Veronica out of temper, and when the fact of having made Veronica cry was enough to put Anne in the best of spirits for several days together. Still, they had always, as cousins, maintained a certain degree of friendly intercourse, and "got on" pretty well together, especially since Anne had had household cares of her own on which to bestow some part of those energies which had aforetime been wont to expend themselves upon other folks' business. But Anne had now the idea firmly fixed in her mind that Veronica had interfered in her management of Kitty; and she clung to it with the tenacity of certain kinds of crabs, which can never leave off pinching whatever they happen to take hold of. The sisters-in-law never met without sundry hints and innuendoes on Anne's part; while, at the same time, she never hesitated to criticize Veronica's treatment of Rosy, even before the child herself.

Veronica's system, if she could be said to have one, was indeed very different from Anne's. She had not nearly so many theories; but then she had a great deal more experience, both in school and at home; and this experience led her to believe that the sooner children learned implicit obedience the better it was both for themselves and those about them. Happily, Rosy had been taught this lesson to some extent even before she was a year old; and Veronica took care that she should not forget it. She did not wish the child ever to remember the time when she had not done as she was told.

"No, no, Rosy," she said, one evening, as the little girl, who had climbed upon a chair, was stretching out her hand towards Mark's wood-carving,—still his favourite evening relaxation,—which lay on the middle of the table. "No, no! Baby must not touch papa's work."

Baby, now getting on towards four years old, looked a little doubtful, and again stretched out her hand towards the forbidden plaything.

"No, no," repeated Veronica, more decidedly. "Does Rosy hear mamma say no?"

"'Ell," said the little one, with a sigh of resignation, "then Rosy wants the Noah's Ark."

"Oh, yes; Rosy may have the Noah's Ark," said Veronica, reaching the plaything in question from the mantel-piece. "Rosy may have her own things; but she must not touch papa's."

"Well, I declare!" said Anne, who was sitting by: "I would not believe there could be so much difference between twin sisters. You would never break Kitty's spirit in that way."

"Rosy's spirit is not broken," replied Veronica. "I do not know a more lively child. She plays and talks from morning till night."

"I cannot help that," persisted Anne. "Her spirit must be broken, or she would never give up so. She will never have any force of character, you will see."

"Because she has learned to obey? I think that is the very reason why she will have it. The sooner children learn that there are things in the world which they cannot do and must not have, the better,—since they must all run against such things, sooner or later."

"Let them enjoy their liberty as long as they can, then. I would rather have Kitty ten times more troublesome than she is, than to see her a poor, tame, spiritless thing, with all the life whipped out of her."

"Do you think Rosy answers that description?"

"Well, perhaps not now; but she will, if you go on as you have begun. I should be afraid to treat a motherless child so, for my part. I should expect the soul of her mother to descend from heaven to defend her."

"I don't believe Daisy will descend from heaven to give Rosy Mark's picture-frame for a plaything," said Veronica, dryly. "In making Rosy docile and obedient, I am only carrying out the work which her own mother began, and I am not afraid of her disapproval. Rosy's enjoyments are not, and will not be, curtailed by any such course: on the contrary, they are increased. A child once thoroughly governed, so as to mind by a word or a look, may be safely indulged to almost any extent; while an ungoverned child must be watched and checked every moment, to prevent it from doing mischief, and, after all, it will be in scrapes half the time."

"Now, Veronica, if you begin to talk at me, I will go," said Anne, who, herself a perfect mistress of the art of insinuation, was always suspecting it in other people. "If you think Kitty such a very bad and troublesome child, I will take care henceforth that she does not come in your way. I suppose all this tirade

The Twin Roses.

"Rosey toddled off, proud of her mission." p. 131.

grows out of the fact that the poor child had the misfortune to break something the last time she was here. If you will tell me the value of the article, I will pay for it."

"Rosy, it is almost time for papa to come home," said Veronica, taking no notice of Anne's remark. "Run and ask Becky for his slippers, and put them by the fire for him."

Rosy toddled off, proud of her mission, which was at once her daily duty and pleasure. The slippers deposited in their place, she began pulling at the chair in which her aunt was seated. Veronica took no notice, wishing to see how the child would manage matters.

"What do you want of my chair, Rosy?" asked Anne.

"Papa's chair, *p'ese*, Aunt Anne," said the little girl. "Put papa's chair by the fire."

"And what will you give me? A kiss?"

"I will say, 'Tinkle, tinkle, 'ittle 'tar,' for you," replied Rosy.

"Dear me, what an inducement! I suppose I must give it up."

She moved as she spoke, and Rosy, putting

forth all her little strength, dragged the chair into its accustomed corner, and was starting off about something else, when Anne said,—

"But stop, Rosy. You promised to say 'Twinkle, twinkle,' for me."

"Yes, you promised, Rosy," said Veronica; "and you must keep your word, you know."

"I want to see Becky make the cakes," pleaded Rosy.

"But you promised," repeated Veronica.

Rosy looked wistfully at the door, but after a moment's pause she turned back, and, planting herself on the hearth-rug, repeated the lines with great emphasis and distinctness.

"Capital!" said Anne. "Do you know any more verses?"

"Yes: I know 'A very young lady,' and 'Thank you, pretty cow,' and the 'House that Jack built,' and 'On Linden.' Becky says that. And I can say my hymns."

"Well, now, run away to Becky, and ask her to bake you a cake, if you like," said Veronica. "We will dispense with any further display of your accomplishments."

"I should think you would be afraid of hurting her head by teaching her so much," said Anne. "The idea of a child of that age learning to repeat 'Hohenlinden'! Of course she cannot understand it."

"Of course not," said Veronica. "No one expects her to do so. But she has a quick ear, and the grand music of the lines took her fancy. She is never tired of hearing verses repeated; and, as Becky's memory is a storehouse of rhymes, new and old, she often entertains Rosy in this way for hours at a time. Rosy picks up the lines which please her ear; and thus, without any attempt made to teach her, she has learned a great many."

"But surely it must be bad to learn so much at her age," persisted Anne. "Precocious children never grow up healthy, either in mind or body."

"My dear Anne, I don't believe 'Nursery-rhymes' or 'Original' poems ever gave any child water on the brain," said Veronica, smiling. "Rosy is no more precocious than any child who lives almost entirely with grown-up people. She is a very sweet, playful little girl, with an active mind, which must needs be employed about something; but even my partiality cannot make me think her a prodigy."

"I expect she will turn out something like that poor little wretch Howard Cowley, who is being paraded about the country," said Anne. "He certainly *is* a prodigy. I never heard any thing like his recitations. They would be remarkable even in a grown person."

"I have not been to see him," said Veronica. "I think all such exhibitions very painful."

"I don't believe he will ever live to grow up," continued Anne. "His head is all out of shape now. I determined when I saw him that Kitty should never be hurt in that way. I think you ought to take warning."

"There is all the difference in the world between allowing a healthy child to learn and repeat verses for her own amusement, and keeping her exhibiting in crowded assembly-rooms till midnight the year round. I would not for the world have my child's health injured; but I do not think her in any present danger."

"Oh, well, of course you know all about it. But will you drive with me to-morrow afternoon? John says I must take the horses out every day, or he will sell them."

"Unluckily, I have an engagement," said Veronica. "On any other day I shall be delighted. But, Anne, if you are going alone, suppose you ask Miss Welles? It is a great pleasure to her to ride, and she seldom has the opportunity; and you know she cannot walk. It would be a real kindness."

"Well, I don't mind if I do," said Anne. "She is a good old soul, if she is rather poky and fussy; and, as you say, it will be a kindness."

Anne went away in a pretty good humour; but the next afternoon, as she was returning from her drive, she met Veronica and Rosy just coming out of the Old Ladies' Asylum.

"So that was the engagement which prevented your driving with me?" said she, as she drew up to the side-walk. "Upon my word, Veronica, I feel flattered!"

"I could not help myself, Anne," replied Veronica. "I promised Miss Brown that I would bring Rosy to see Beauty's puppies, and I promised Rosy that she should come."

"Rosy, indeed!" said Anne, scornfully. "Who minds a promise to a baby?"

"Rosy is not exactly a baby," replied Veronica; "and, if I did not mind my promises to her, I should have little reason to suppose that she would regard hers to me. You are mistaken if you think I would not keep an engagement to Rosy or Kitty as quickly as to a grown person."

"Oh, very well. Drive on, William."

"I want to go with Aunt Roney!" cried Kitty, who was very fond of her **aunt** Veronica, — perhaps because she was the only person in the world who ever governed her.

"No; you cannot go to-night. Aunt Roney does not want you."

"Yes, she does. Don't you, auntie?"

"To be sure I want you, if mamma is willing,—not else. Do let her come, Anne. I will send Becky home with her."

"I cannot allow it," said Anne, who, like her husband, now and then took a brief spasm of authority. "I have said no, and that is enough. Drive on, William."

Kitty kicked, screamed, and roared with all her might, much to the discomfiture of poor, precise Miss Welles, who did not at all relish driving through the principal streets of the city in such company.

Veronica pursued her way with Rosy, and presently saw Anne's carriage draw up to the side-walk and wait for her to come up. Kitty was still roaring and kicking.

"Veronica, if you don't mind being troubled

with Kitty, I really wish you would take her," said Anne, colouring a little. "I cannot drive through the Avenue with the child in this state. I will send for her by-and-by."

Miss Welles looked amazed at this specimen of family government. Veronica suppressed her smiles as well as she could, and took possession of Kitty, who, having gained her point, stopped crying directly, and was as placid as possible. She enjoyed her visit highly, and never thought of crying, even when forbidden to pull the tail and ears of Nero, now a consequential and dignified cat.

"Well, Kittens," said John Campion, when she returned home, "what did auntie say to you?"

"She said, 'No, no, Kitty!'" said the little girl, seriously.

"Indeed! And what did you say? Did you scream?"

"No," said Kitty. "I was a good girl. Auntie said so."

"And do you like to be good?"

"No," replied Kitty, still more seriously. "I don't always like to be good and not touch Uncle Mark's things."

"That is it, exactly," said Anne. "'Don't

touch!' is Veronica's first, second, and third commandment. She makes a regular little slave of Rosy."

"She takes her **slavery very easily**," remarked John. "I never saw a livelier or happier child. And as to the not-touching system, I think it a very convenient one. Kitty is really very troublesome in that respect. I think she is old enough to learn to let things alone."

"She is nothing but a baby, Mr. Campion. I think it is absurd for you to expect her to behave like a grown woman. Such wonderfully perfect children never live to grow up. I do not believe Rosy will ever see twelve years in the world."

"She seems healthy enough, for all I see."

"That is because you men don't understand such matters. Her head is all out of shape now; and no wonder, considering the way she is drilled and crammed all day long. I shall speak to Mark about it."

"You had better not. Mark won't relish any interference, I can tell you. He thinks his wife perfection."

"They need not interfere with me, then," said Anne, peevishly. "I shall never get over

Veronica's going and talking to you about Kitty's dress, that first winter."

"What upon earth are you talking about?" asked John, in great amazement. "Veronica talk to me about the child's dress? What could put such a notion into your head?"

"Oh, well, if you choose to deny it, I shall not contradict you; but I know she did. You would never have thought of such a thing if some one had not put you up to it."

"Nonsense!" said John, gruffly: "as if any person of common sense could not see that a white frock and short sleeves were not a fit dress for a child in cold weather! Veronica never said a word about the matter, nor any one else."

"Oh, well, have it your own way," said Anne. "Come, Kitty; it is time to go to bed." But Kitty had no notion of going to bed, and, as usual, carried her point of sitting up, till she fell asleep in her chair.

CHAPTER VII.

NELLY.

THE next year passed along very quietly with our friends. Mark's book was published, and turned out a decided success. Edition after edition was called for; the book was well spoken of in the Reviews, and the great monthlies competed with each other in compliments, and requests for contributions. Money flowed in upon the family in South Street, and Mark found himself for the first time in case to fulfil the cherished wish of his heart. He added a room to his house for a library, and bought the vacant lot next him for a garden. John ridiculed the idea of the library, but approved of the purchase as a good investment, since land in that neighbourhood was rapidly rising in value. Anne thought the library a good thing, since it would take the litter of Mark's books and papers out of the sitting-room; but she thought the garden great nonsense, and prophesied that Veronica would never be able to keep any flowers, with a child of Rosy's age running about. As to vegetables, every one knew that it cost twice as much to raise as to buy them.

"That depends," said Mark. "If one hires all the labour done, a garden is doubtless a very expensive affair; but I expect to do the greater part of the work myself, with what help Veronica and Rosy can give me. I shall not aspire very high at present, but I think we may compass some radishes and salad, tomatoes and cucumbers, and perhaps a few string-beans. Such things taste very differently when they come directly from the garden to the table, from what they do when brought three or four miles to market. Then I mean to have some raspberries and currants, grape-vines, and a cherry-tree or two, and perhaps some dwarf pears,—though the last are rather too easily stolen to be entirely satisfactory."

"You will never succeed in the world," said Anne. "What are you planting now? Corn? What an idea!"

"Popping-corn, to amuse Rosy and Rosy's papa in the winter evenings."

"What a child you are, Mark! You will never be any thing else, I do believe."

"Never, so far as popped corn is concerned, unless I lose my teeth; and, really, I don't see why I should."

"Well, I should think a man who had been favourably noticed in the Reviews might be above such child's-play."

"I don't seem to find myself so much changed by the praise of the Reviews," said Mark, putting on a look of deep consideration. "Have you observed any alteration in me, Veronica?"

"Really, I cannot say," replied Veronica, laughing. "Becky says the last jug of syrup has gone off faster than usual, and that she cannot keep any cakes unless she hides them; but that last is an old complaint. I think you take more sugar in your coffee than you did,—which, at the present price, is not a sign of increasing wisdom."

Anne looked seriously annoyed. She never could understand the kind of pleasant rallying which was constantly passing between Mark and his wife, and always suspected them of laughing at her. "You are a pair of babies," said she, "and you will never be any thing else. I should think you had had trouble enough to sober you."

"My dear sister, we have had trouble enough to teach us not to borrow any more, but to take and enjoy every innocent pleasure our kind Father sends us, even if it be no more than popping corn," said Mark, more gravely. "I believe one great secret of a happy life consists in finding pleasure in little things. I am sorry you think I am not sufficiently dignified to be praised by the Reviews, but I hope you will not be seriously afflicted by it, for I am sadly afraid I shall never be any better."

"And there is Rosy, now. Do you expect you are ever going to teach her to let your things alone?"

"I hope so," said Veronica. "She is very good about meddling in the house. I dare say I may have some little trouble at first; but I think she will soon learn."

"Yes, after she has been whipped and sent to bed a dozen times. I should rather never have a garden than to pay such a price for it."

"What a lively imagination you have,

Anne! Rosy never was whipped in her life. I hope you don't report your ideas of my family government as facts. People will think me a domestic tyrant."

Anne coloured a little, for she was conscious of having more than once enlarged upon her sister's system as compared with her own. She had even written to her mother-in-law such an account of Veronica's severity that Mrs. Campion was quite alarmed, and thought seriously of remonstrating with Veronica upon the subject.

The family in South Street passed a pleasant summer, in spite of bricks and mortar, dust and noise, and all the discomforts of building. Mark worked in his garden early and late, and, like the fabled giant of the Greek story, drew health and strength of body and mind from contact with mother earth. His was a mind exquisitely alive to every beauty, whether of nature or art. Veronica's portulacca-bed, opening its many-coloured blossoms to the sun, was a constant feast to him; and every little bird or beetle was like a personal friend. Every new flower was to him, who lived habitually so near to God, like a new gift from that beneficent Friend of whom and for whom are all things. The lilies spoke to him their lesson of faith, and the vine told of Him who is the true vine. Yes, Mark was very happy in his garden. Veronica could not quite reach to Mark's enthusiasm. Hers was a mind of another stamp; but she loved flowers and the work they involved, and she spent many happy and healthful hours in weeding and trimming, in transplanting and layering, in training Virginia creepers and convolvulus in the way they should go. Rosy toddled about after mamma, dug in her own peculiar corner, exclaimed, "Pretty! pretty!" over every new blossom, and imagined she was making herself useful in picking up sticks and dragging away stones in her little cart.

Veronica, while working in the garden, had several times noticed a thin, odd-looking child, some six or seven years old, peeping through the open fence which bounded the bottom of the garden. Happening one day to be at work close by, she entered into conversation with the child, and asked her name.

"Nelly Wicks," was the reply. Veronica recognized the name as belonging to a poor, unfortunate Scotchman, a man of some literary pretensions and some real talent, who had

K

fallen from one grade of dissipation to another, and finally died a victim to brandy. He had left a wife and three children, the oldest of whom was supporting himself respectably in a printing-office. Mark had procured the place for him; and the lad had persisted in accepting it, much to the disgust of his father and mother, who suffered from that sort of gentility which considers all mechanical employment vulgar. The second child was little Nelly, and there was a younger child about three years old. Mrs. Wicks was supported partly by a small annuity paid her by her husband's family, partly by fine work and knitting, which she did very skilfully when she could make up her mind to do it at all.

"And how old are you, Nelly?" asked Veronica, continuing the conversation.

"Six," replied Nelly; "and Molly is three."

"Do you love flowers, Nelly?"

"Yes, ma'am,—very much."

"Would you like to come into the garden and see the flowers?" Nelly's eyes sparkled. "Well, you may come; but you must be careful not to touch any thing."

This was the first of Nelly's visits. The next day she came again, and brought with her Molly, a pretty but spoiled little imp, as pert as Nelly was shy and timid. Veronica watched them closely without appearing to do so, and presently she saw Molly pull off a rosebud.

"Don't, Molly! You mustn't touch the lady's flowers," said Nelly.

"I will, too!" screamed Molly. "I will have a flower! I'll tell mother."

"Hush, hush!" said Veronica: "that will never do. Molly, if you touch my flowers I shall send you out of the garden."

Molly screamed louder, and Veronica, taking her in her arms, set her over the fence into her own premises. Molly ran roaring to her mother, who presently appeared, calling Nelly in a tone of voice which of itself was enough to drive the best child in the world into thoughts of rebellion. No sooner was the child within reach than she was greeted with a box on the ear which nearly threw her down.

"You wicked child! How dare you push your little sister down and kick her?"

"I didn't!" sobbed Nelly. "She wanted to pick the lady's flowers."

"Don't talk to me, you bad child!—don't!" said Mrs. Wicks, for the first time perceiving that she had an auditor. "Nelly is a very naughty child, ma'am," she continued, addressing herself to Veronica. "She makes me a great deal of trouble."

"I am sorry to hear it," replied Veronica. "However, she certainly was not to blame in this case. She only attempted, by the gentlest means, to prevent Molly from picking my flowers."

"She slapped me and kicked me!" cried Molly.

"She neither slapped nor kicked you," said Veronica. "I am afraid *you* are a naughty girl, since you tell lies about your little sister."

"Molly is only a baby," said Mrs. Wicks. "We do not expect her to have much sense; but Nelly is old enough to know better, and she is a very bad child. Her poor, dear papa often said so."

"He didn't!" sobbed Nelly. "Papa was good to me."

"You see for yourself, ma'am. But come into the house this minute, Nelly, and do your sewing. Come, darling" (to Molly): "mamma will give her a piece of cake."

"I won't!" roared Molly. "I want to go in the lady's garden."

"I cannot have you in my garden," said Veronica. "I never allow children in my garden who meddle with what does not belong to them."

Molly went off crying, and for a day or two Veronica saw no more of either of the children.

After a while, however, Nelly was again seen peeping through the gate, and Veronica invited her in. Presently Molly came also, demanding admittance.

"No," said Veronica: "I never have meddling children about me; and I will tell you another thing, Molly: if you cry, I will never let you come into the garden again, as long as you live."

Molly's roar stopped as suddenly as a stream of water when the faucet is turned. She remained looking wistfully through the gate, till Veronica, having finished her labours, said to Nelly,—

"I am going in now: so you had better run home. Here are some flowers for you; and here is one for you, Molly."

Molly took the offered marigold and ran off with a beaming face to show it to her mother. She seemed to find the new sensation of being good rather an agreeable one; for she returned the next day, and, being allowed to come in, behaved as well as possible, running about after Veronica and Rosy, and chatting to them both as good-naturedly as possible till Nelly came after her. Then she made up a face to cry; but a warning look from Veronica restrained her, and she went off quietly enough.

It soon became an established custom for the children to visit the garden every evening. Mrs. Wicks seemed rather pleased by Veronica's notice of them, and even attempted to establish a gossiping sort of intimacy,—an attempt which was not in the least encouraged. Mark did not at all relish her familiarities; and one evening, as she bolted into the sitting-room without knocking, he asked her, rather significantly,—

"Is the bell out of order, Mrs. Wicks? I did not hear you ring."

Mrs. Wicks took the hint, and the next time rang the bell. Becky went to the door.

"Is Mrs. Campion at home?" asked Mrs. Wicks.

"Yes: she is at home, but she is busy," said Becky, with whom Mrs. Wicks was no favourite. "Did you want any thing in particular?"

"No,—nothing in particular," replied Mrs. Wicks, rather taken aback; "only to sit a while. Is my Nelly here?"

"Yes; she's sitting on the back-steps, having a quiet, comfortable time," said Becky. "You had better leave her alone, unless **you want** her particularly."

"No; I don't want her if she is not in mischief. She is such a bad child that **I am** never h'easy about her a minute."

"Then you had better leave her alone; for she is as good as possible here," returned Becky; and, so saying, she shut the door.

Mrs. Wicks had also certain principles which regulated her family government, one of which was a kind of reversal of the old law of primogeniture. The youngest child for the time-being could do no wrong. He was an absolute monarch, to whom every one else, and especially his elder brothers and sisters, **were** to bow down in absolute submission. Each of the children in turn had enjoyed this dangerous eminence, had been indulged in all sorts of mischief, and laughed at and applauded for every piece of impudence. As soon as another baby came, the last monarch was dethroned, and soon found himself snubbed and punished for the very tricks which he had been taught to think pretty and cunning. Mrs. Wicks's other grand principle was that children were always to be found fault with, and never on any account to be praised, especially before strangers. Every visitor she had, was entertained with an account of Nelly's misdeeds, especially if the little girl were in the room,—till many people pitied the poor woman extremely, for having such a graceless child. Two unfortunate consequences resulted from this system. One was that the child, finding herself equally blamed whether she did well or ill, soon made up her mind that there was no use in trying to please her mother, and that she might just as well take her own way and please herself. The other consequence Veronica herself remarked to Mrs. Wicks one day when that wise woman had been more than usually diffuse before a lady who came to order some work.

"Mrs. Wicks," said she, when Nelly left the room, "do you ever reflect that you are establishing a bad reputation for that child, which she will never get over?"

Mrs. Wicks looked a little scared.

"You tell every one what a bad child she is," continued Veronica. "Presently you will lead people to think she is quite a monster of iniquity; and you will find the character will stick to her in such a way as seriously to affect her prospects in life. Suppose you were to be taken away suddenly: who would be willing to give Nelly a home?"

"Nelly does not care any thing about being scolded," said Mrs. Wicks, "but it does shame her a little to be found fault with before company."

"And how long do you think that will last? But, Mrs. Wicks, since blame does Nelly no good, suppose you try a little praise. That would be a novelty, and would perhaps answer a good purpose."

But Mrs. Wicks thought it would never do to praise children. They always presumed upon it, and Nelly was sure to do so. She was a very cold-hearted child, and did not love her little sister in the least. Veronica thought it no wonder that Nelly did not love her sister, seeing how the child was allowed to interfere in every way with her comfort,—to spoil her playthings, tear her books, and pound her on the least provocation, besides being encouraged to tell tales of her on every occasion. There was, however, no use in talking to Mrs. Wicks, who was wiser in her own conceit than ten men who could render a reason: so Veronica contented herself with affording Nelly as many happy hours as possible within her own premises. The child needed very little to make her happy. She was perfectly contented with being allowed to creep into the parlour in the twilight after Rosy was in bed, and sit at Veronica's feet, sometimes fondling her hands, and now and then asking some odd question, which showed how full and running over with thoughts was her little, untaught mind. Presently Mark began to notice the shy little girl, to answer her questions, and to talk to her in the peculiarly quiet and soothing strain which he so well understood. Nelly had been considered rather a dunce in school; she had not got on well with her books; and, on inquiry, Veronica found she had never learned to write.

"You are not going to school now, Nelly," said she. "If you like to come over every morning at nine o'clock, I will give you a writing-lesson and hear you spell, and we will see if we cannot get a good start before school begins again."

Nelly joyfully assented, and made her appearance punctually at the time appointed. She acquitted herself very well for some days, and went home quite happy. The third or fourth morning, Molly made her appearance, and stayed all through the lesson-hour, effectually distracting Nelly's attention. Veronica took no notice the first day; but the next morning, finding the same thing repeated, she said to Nelly,—

"Nelly, you must not bring Molly with you when you come to say your lesson."

"Mother said I shouldn't come unless Molly did, because Molly cried," said the child, hanging her head.

"I cannot help that," said Veronica. "You must tell your mother that I cannot have Molly in the morning. She is quite too troublesome, and hinders you from doing any thing properly."

"I'll tell her what you say," replied Nelly; "but I 'most know she won't let me come without Molly. I have finished my copy, Mrs. Campion."

"That is very neatly done, Nelly. It is the

best we have seen yet. You must have taken great pains."

Nelly's pale face flushed and brightened, as she answered, "I knew *you* would say it was well done, because it *was* well done."

"Poor little young one!" said Becky, to whom Veronica repeated Nelly's remark. "She knows what justice is when she gets it, anyhow. But what is the use of her trying to do any thing at home? That woman finds fault with her whether she does right or wrong, and the child has no motive to be good. She does well enough over here, and minds with the first word; but she does misbehave at home, —and no wonder."

"We must try by degrees to give her a higher motive than any human praise, even her mother's," said Veronica. "I remember an anecdote that Daisy Brush told me, which made a strong impression on me. Daisy was talking to Chloe, the old negro woman who took care of her, and who seems to have been about her only friend, and lamenting the impossibility of pleasing Miss Brush, whatever she did.

"'Honey,' said Chloe, 'you can't please her. No one ever could please Miss Addy,—no, not an angel from heaven; and the heavenlier he was, the worse she would treat him. When I first came here, I used to wear my heart out trying to suit her; and the more I tried, the more she aggravated me, till I used to think she would drive me out of my mind. Finally, one day, I thought to myself, There's no use in trying to please Miss Addy, 'cause she won't be pleased, nohow; but there's One I can please, 'cause He sees my heart and He knows what I try to do. So I left off trying to please Miss Addy, and went to work with all my might to please God and do what I thought he'd like.'

" 'And did that do her any good?' asked Daisy.

" 'No, honey; I can't say it did; but it did me a sight of good, and I've felt better ever since.' "

"Poor old soul!" said Becky. "I wonder what I should do if I were in her place? I wonder which would have the worst time,— me or my mistress?"

CHAPTER VIII.

DEATH.

WE must now pass hastily over three or four years in the life of our friends in South Street and on the Avenue, and proceed to a period of more importance.

Mark's book passed through more editions, and the second part was eagerly looked for and heartily welcomed. The increase of fame brought with it an equally agreeable increase of fortune; and, Mark's time being fully taken up with such work as he liked best, he gave up much of the drudgery which had heretofore occupied him, and spent a great deal of his time at home.

The new library had already lost its look of newness, and the shelves which looked so bare and empty when first put up were crowded three-deep with volumes of all sorts and sizes. The dwarf pear-trees in the new garden had come into fine bearing; while the raspberry and strawberry **plantations** reproved Anne's want of faith by full crops of berries.

Rosy had grown, with every thing else. She was now shooting up into a tall girl, getting her second teeth, and losing much of her remarkable infantine beauty. Despite Anne's predictions,—despite Veronica's shocking presumption in teaching the child to read at four years old, and to write at five,—Rosy was neither rickety nor hump-backed, neither idiotic nor epileptic. On the contrary, her health, naturally delicate, had constantly improved under her mother's careful nursing, till she was now as healthy and sturdy as any child in the city. Growing up in an atmosphere of books, she of course "took to them," as Becky said, from her earliest years. She was not more than three years old when she announced her intention to make books like papa; and, as she could not use a pen, she was constantly begging her mother or Becky to write down her stories for her. All her tales were of course highly moral, and inflicted terrific punishment upon offenders, as in the case of the wicked boy who *would* throw stones at the chickens, and was afterwards carried off and devoured by *ostriches*,—

they being the biggest birds with which Rosy was acquainted.

After she learned to read, books were a never-failing source of enjoyment to her. Becky had early made her acquainted with some of her own favourites in prose and verse; and "The Lady of the Lake," "The Minstrel," "The Pilgrim's Progress," and "Bishop Heber's Journals," afforded Rosy new delight when she came to study them for herself. Of course, much was not understood; but Veronica had an idea that it did not hurt children to read books beyond their comprehension. Rosy's juvenile library was a very large one, —thanks to the liberality of Mr. Clarendon, Mark's partner, who never allowed her to visit the store without giving her the choice of a large assortment of books; and her favourites were read and re-read until fairly worn out.

Veronica had taught her to take good care of her books; and the few torn pages and battered covers were mostly due to Kitty, whose lawlessness was not always to be restrained even by Aunt Veronica.

Rosy had never been to school, as her mother had plenty of time to bestow upon her at home. She had never been driven, and she had enjoyed a great deal of out-of-door exercise; yet at eight years old she could read as well as any one, write a tolerable hand, spell most common words correctly (a somewhat rare accomplishment in these days, by the way), and she had begun to learn lessons in mental arithmetic and grammar. The latter study, usually so dry and wearisome to children, Veronica taught her by word of mouth; and Rosy could point out the nouns, verbs, and adjectives in a sentence, could tell whether the verbs were regular or irregular, and what they governed, long before she had even looked into a grammar. Her lesson-times were short, rarely exceeding fifteen or twenty minutes at one time; but Veronica tolerated no trifling, and insisted upon Rosy's bestowing her full powers of mind on the subject for the time-being. It is not to be supposed that all these lessons were gotten over without some trouble on both sides. Rosy was sometimes idle and sometimes careless, and now and then required a certain amount of coercion, as most children do; but, on the whole, the tasks were a source of enjoyment to both pupil and teacher.

The little girl's moral and religious education advanced at the same time with that of

L

her mind. As we have seen, she early learned to obey with a word or look. She had been taught, as soon as she could walk, to exert her small strength for the benefit of others, and to find pleasure in so doing. Her first patch-work resulted in a kettle-holder for Miss Brown, and a chair-cushion for Aunt Phœbe Ray, an old coloured woman who was a frequent and welcome visitor in Becky's kitchen. Her pennies were hoarded to buy Christmas-presents for everybody; and she found much more pleasure in laying them out in this way than she would have done in spending them selfishly upon herself. She was taught to tell the truth on the smallest occasion, to be polite and kind to every one, whether rich or poor, to study the comfort of those about her, and to deny herself for their sakes.

As soon as Rosy was old enough to speak,— long before she could speak plainly,—Veronica taught her to say her prayers, and to know to whom she was speaking. Mark was never so busy that he did not spare half an hour before Rosy's bedtime, to take her in his arms and talk to her, in gentle, reverent tones, of her Father in heaven, who gave her all that she loved, of the dear Saviour, the Son of God, who came down to earth and died and rose again for her salvation; of the Holy Spirit, to whom she must look for help against her sins, and comfort in her sorrows. All the great realities of our holy religion were so early impressed on Rosy's memory that she could not recollect when she had not known something of them; and Mark's earnest, living spirit of devotion made his instructions realities. This twilight hour was very precious to Rosy and to Rosy's papa, and served to draw closer the bond between them. If the little one had done any thing wrong during the day, it was confessed at this time, with tears and promises of amendment; if she had met with any trouble, it was then poured into papa's ready ear, sure to meet with sympathy and comfort. It was not always by any means convenient for Mark to spare this half-hour; but he would have sacrificed a great deal, rather than have given up his particular share in his little daughter's education.

It is not to be supposed, with all this, that Rosy was altogether a faultless child. She was sometimes idle and sometimes careless; she had rather a quick temper, and she was prone somewhat to dwell upon and brood over small offences and troubles. Nevertheless, she was a very good little girl, and her early-acquired habits of amusing herself independently and letting other people's things alone made her an unusually pleasant child to live with.

Anne's training, like Veronica's, had produced its legitimate results, and Kitty at eight years old was pronounced, by all her acquaintances, the most thoroughly spoiled child in the city. A little torment, an intolerable nuisance, she was called by the servants and visitors; and such she undoubtedly was. Anne had always made herself a slave to Kitty, attending assiduously to all her motions, gratifying her every whim, no matter at what inconvenience to herself, and allowing the child to find fault with and criticize her to her heart's content. Everybody and every thing in the house was made to give way to Kitty. Whatever she wanted, that she had, if it was to be found; if not, some substitute must be provided. If she flew into a passion, she was to be coaxed into good humour again; if she cried, she was to be pacified; if she condescended to learn at all, she was to be praised and petted as though she had performed something marvellous; if she refused to learn, she was not to be driven, for fear she should be led to dislike study, or lest her health should be injured by over-application.

Anne hoped by all this indulgence to win the child's love, and, as she said, influence her by the means of her affections; but she made a singular mistake. Kitty had very little regard for her mother, and no respect whatever. The following is a specimen of scenes which were constantly occurring between the mother and daughter. Kitty had been playing with her blocks and dishes, and was going out of the room, leaving them strewed all over the carpet.

"Come, Kitty; put your blocks away, like a good girl."

"I don't want to."

"Oh, yes; put them away nicely. Kitty will be a good, kind girl, and put the things away for mamma: won't she?"

"I sha'n't. I want to go in the garden."

"Oh, I see: Kitty don't love mamma. Poor mamma! Come, put away the things, and mamma will read her a pretty story."

"I don't want a story. I want to go in the garden."

"Well, I will show you papa's great book

of animals. Doesn't Kitty want to see the pretty squirrels and bears?"

If the bribe was sufficient, Kitty would sometimes condescend **to do** as she was entreated; but more generally she went on her **own way**, and the blocks were put up by some one else. Kitty was allowed to eat what she liked, to get up and go to bed when she liked, **to go** out or not when she pleased. She was **never** taught **to deny** herself any gratification of her appetite, lest **she** should attach too much importance to **eating** and drinking, **or** to suppress any speech, however impertinent or foolish, **lest** she should learn to be artful. She was never **taught** to have any care of her clothes and playthings; **and,** indeed, the principal use she made of **her** toys was to break them.

At eight years old, Kitty was thoughtless, exacting, self-indulgent, and **so** thoroughly *blasée* (I would use an English word if I could find one which expressed my meaning **so exactly**) to all sorts of indulgences and amusements, that **no one of** them could afford her pleasure for more than a few minutes at a time. She respected but three people in the world,— her father, and her uncle and aunt, all of whom she found herself obliged to defer to. She loved her father and Rosy dearly, and scarcely any one else. Her health was injured by her irregular hours and habits of eating, and, like Rosy, she was fast losing her childish beauty.

For a long time Anne could see nothing but perfection in Kitty; but during the last year or two her eyes had been a little opened. She could not help observing the difference between the two girls whenever they were brought together, and perceiving that the advantage was not upon Kitty's side. At first this conviction showed itself in pettishness towards Rosy and her mother, and in a strong disposition to magnify any little thing which the child said or did amiss; but by degrees the pettishness began to turn upon Kitty herself. Then came an attempt to govern the child,—to break her spirit, as Anne phrased it. But Kitty's spirit, not having been bent at the right time, was hard to break now. Her will, like Rosy's, was naturally strong; and, unlike Rosy's, it had never been taught to give way. Kitty came off conqueror in the struggle by dint of sheer screaming and kicking; and, after a prolonged contest, Anne was fain to purchase peace and quietness by a double share of indulgence.

But Anne's pride was now alarmed. It could not be denied that Veronica's system had succeeded in making Rosy a much more agreeable child than Kitty,—that she was more forward, better-mannered, healthier, and, by consequence, prettier. She made up her mind that it was time to take Kitty seriously in hand and break her in.

She did not find the task an easy one; nor was she particularly well qualified to perform it, never having been very well broken in herself. Nevertheless did she persevere in her intention. The nursery now became the daily scene of battles loud and long between Kitty and her mother,—the one commanding, the other crying and resisting, till either Anne grew tired and abandoned the contest, or Kitty, subdued by sheer physical force of shaking and whipping, did as she was told, to be pitied, comforted, and secretly indulged by Jane, as soon as her mother was out of sight, and usually to rebel again at the first opportunity.

Anne was not very judicious, and was just as likely to provoke a battle about some perfectly indifferent matter as about a fault of consequence. Then Kitty's offended sense of justice gave double force to her resistance, and she was often perfectly frantic with rage, being on one occasion only withheld by force from throwing herself out of the window.

Treated in this way, Kitty grew sullen, sly, and morose, and lost the few engaging qualities she possessed. Anne began to find her troublesome, tiresome, a little plague, an ungrateful child, and to talk seriously of sending her to boarding-school.

From her father, Kitty was sure of receiving even-handed justice; but, unfortunately for her, Mr. Campion was from home a great part of the time. He had been called to the presidency of a railroad company whose affairs were sadly entangled, and which he was expected to put in order; for he was a man in whose integrity and business capacity every one placed the utmost confidence; and he found his hands so full that he had very little time to spend at home.

Kitty was always good and happy with her father, whose will she had early learned was law. All was sunshine when he appeared, and he had, consequently, very little notion of how matters were going between his wife and daughter. Whenever Kitty could obtain permission

P

to spend the day with her aunt, she was satisfied; since Veronica, though she never unduly indulged her, or allowed her to tyrannize over Rosy, was always just and kind; but Anne's jealousy of her sister-in-law had not decreased with years, and was called into active exercise by Kitty's affection for her: so that these visits were not so frequent as formerly. Such was the state of things at the time we resume the thread of our tale.

Dinner was over in South Street. Mark had assumed his favourite chair and his dressing-gown; but he did not seem to throw off his cares as usual, but looked thoughtful and anxious. Rosy, now promoted to the dignity of sitting up till eight o'clock, was busy in a corner with Nelly Wicks, setting out the doll's table for a grand dinner-party; for she was still very young in her enjoyments, and loved her dolls as well as ever. Veronica's fingers were busy with her knitting, and her eyes were fixed thoughtfully on the fire.

"Veronica," said Mark, after an interval of silence, "have you seen John lately?"

"Not very lately,—no!" replied Veronica, rousing herself from her abstraction. "Now I think of it, I have seen him only once in several weeks, and then only for a few minutes. He is away a great deal, you know."

"Then you have not seen him since he came home this last time?"

"No. Why?"

"I think he's looking very unwell," said Mark, gravely. "I fear he is sadly overworking himself with this railroad business."

"I suppose it *is* very perplexing," returned Veronica. "I noticed no change in him the last time I met him, except that he seemed rather more abstracted than usual."

"I went into the office to see him this afternoon, and really I was startled," said Mark. "He hardly seemed to know me till I spoke to him, and his hand shook like an old man's. I wish he could be prevailed upon to lay down his business cares for a time and rest. He told me this afternoon that his head often felt strangely, and that he had been trying to see the doctor, but had not found time."

Mark had hardly finished speaking, when some one hastily opened the side door, and Becky was heard to exclaim, in a tone of great surprise,—

"Why, Kitty, child, what brings you here at this time of night?"

"What can be the matter?" asked Veronica, turning pale, and rising to open the door; but, before she reached it, Kitty rushed in, much excited.

"Oh, Uncle Mark, do come to our house directly! papa is very sick, and mamma is not at home!" And, overcome with grief, she burst into hysterical sobs.

While Mark hastily assumed his coat and boots, Veronica tried to soothe the child, and to obtain from her some account of her father's illness.

"Mamma went away to the concert, and papa said he could not go, because his head ached, and he wanted to be quiet; and he was leaning back in his great chair, and when I spoke to him he did not answer. And his face looks dreadful, and he does not know any thing at all!"

"Have you sent for the doctor?"

"Yes: Charles went for him; but he did not come back, and so I came after you."

"Can you come, Veronica?" asked Mark. She was ready in a moment. She would have had Kitty remain with Rosy; but the child was not willing to stay away from her father, and Veronica did not urge the point. They found the doctor at the house; but there was nothing to be done. The first attack had been the fatal blow, and Anne arrived at home only in time to see her husband breathe his last.

Kitty was like a mad creature. She had never been taught to put any restraint upon herself, and she loved her father better than any thing else in the world. Veronica tried to quiet her by telling her how much she would increase her mother's grief; but Kitty had never been taught to consider other people's feelings, and the argument had no weight with her. She clung to her father's body, struck furiously at those who approached her, and was finally carried away by main force and put to bed. At last, exhausted by the violence of her emotions, she sobbed herself to sleep.

Anne's grief was almost as violent as Kitty's, and, as usual, she sought relief in thinking some one was to blame. She could not believe but that something might have been done, and she alternately reproached Mark, the doctor, herself for being absent, and John for not having told her how ill he was. Veronica listened and soothed, with unvarying gentleness and patience, till at last Anne seemed struck with some sense of her own ungraciousness.

"It is too bad for me to keep you up, Veronica. I know, of course, that you and Mark did all that you could; but it does seem so hard that he should be taken so suddenly without any time for preparation or any thing. And what will people think of me?—being away at a concert when my husband was dying!"

"Every one will know how sudden the attack was," said Veronica, soothingly; "and as for preparation, Anne, I hope and trust that John's was not put off till a dying hour."

"No: I didn't mean that," sobbed Anne. "He was always good and religious,—always; but, then, to think of his leaving his affairs all unsettled, and I don't know any thing about business,—and I shall be left so lonely!"

"There is Kitty, you know," said Veronica. "Poor child, she has been almost beside herself!"

"Yes; she loved him dearly. She would always mind him when she did not care for any one else. Where is she? I want her with me."

"She is asleep," replied Veronica. "I hardly think it will be safe to wake her."

But Anne, like Kitty, had never learned to

control herself. She insisted upon going to see the child, awaked her by her sobs, and then, as Veronica had foreseen, there was a repetition of the distressing scene. She was at last obliged to call Mark, who, exerting the authority which he well knew how to assume, sent Anne to bed in one room and Kitty in another, holding the little girl in her arms till she fell asleep. When she awoke, the violence of her grief seemed to have passed off; but it was replaced by a settled melancholy, painful to witness in so young a child. She wept no more, but moped silently about the house, unable to amuse or employ herself, and keeping as much as possible out of the way of her mother, whose bursts of weeping seemed to irritate her beyond endurance. She rejected, ungraciously enough, her aunt's offer to take her home or to bring Rosy to keep her company, and seemed to find her only consolation in sitting in her father's room and turning over and arranging his little pieces of personal property,—the seals and pens upon his desk, and the eye-glass, cigar-case, and smoking-apparatus, which he had been used to keep on a little table by his arm-chair.

"There is a wonderful intensity of character

in that little thing," said Mark to Veronica, one day. "It seems as if almost any thing might be made of her, if one only knew where to begin."

"She has great force of character," replied Veronica; "and therein lies my one hope for her. If she were a fool, I should say she was thoroughly spoiled; but I hope she may yet have sense enough to correct her own errors. The worst thing about her is the selfishness in which she has been systematically trained. She cares for nothing and nobody but herself, now that her father is gone. I fear she has a great deal of trouble before her, poor child; for, between ourselves, I doubt Anne's having much patience with her faults, now they have become troublesome, even though they are in a great measure the work of her own hands."

"Kitty is losing her beauty, too," observed Mark. "How very thin and dark she has grown!"

"She will outgrow that," replied Veronica. "I think she will turn out a very handsome woman."

"Where is she now?"

"Sitting in John's room, keeping watch over his property. She will not allow the housemaid to touch any thing, but has fairly tired herself out in attempting to sweep and dust the room herself. I told them to let her have her own way; for I thought exercise the best thing for her. Poor child! she may well mourn, for she has lost her best friend, one on whom she might have relied through all changes. John's faithfulness was one of his strong points. He was as firm as a rock."

CHAPTER IX.

FARTHER CHANGES.

JOHN'S affairs turned out to be in perfect order. His property was much larger than any one supposed, and all was well and profitably invested. His will, dated very soon after his marriage, left twenty-five thousand dollars to his mother, the same sum to Mark, a thousand dollars and a small house in the suburbs to " my old and respected friend Miss Rebecca Owen," various large legacies to the different charitable institutions in the city, and the remainder, amounting to more than ninety thousand dollars, to his wife. There was a codicil, dated nearly seven years back, by which ten thousand dollars was left to Kitty under Mr. Clarendon's guardianship; but it was not signed.

" He must have written it immediately after

the conversation we had upon the subject," said Mark. "I am very sorry it was not signed."

"Do you think it a good plan to make children independent of their parents?" asked Mr. Clarendon, who was one of the executors.

"Not usually; but the present case is rather a peculiar one."

Mr. Clarendon looked over his glasses, and nodded two or three times significantly. "You mean that Mrs. Campion is a young and pretty woman, and, the property being left altogether in her own power, she is likely enough to——" Another significant nod closed the sentence.

Mark nodded in return. "There is one thing about it," said he. "I shall now be able to make a home for Kitty, if any thing should occur to render it necessary."

"Well, Mark, I must say that's very unselfish in you. Kitty is a thoroughly spoiled little monkey. I don't think I ever saw her match. I should not like to be the one to undertake her."

"My wife has a great knack at managing children," said Mark; "and Kitty has so much sense and force at the bottom of all her faults, that I cannot think hers a hopeless case. However, there is no use in borrowing trouble."

Anne was considerably disappointed in her husband's will. She had made up her mind that every thing would be left to her, and, though she was certainly very well provided for, having an income of over six thousand a year, she felt herself very much aggrieved that so large a share of her husband's property should have been given to Mrs. Campion and Mark.

"I can't understand it at all," she said to Mr. Clarendon. "John never had any opinion of Mark as a business man; and it passes my comprehension how he could have been willing to put such a large sum of money into his hands."

"Mark is not exactly a money-making man, though he has made a very pretty sum out of that book of his," observed Mr. Clarendon; "but, as far as punctuality and exactness go, he is as good a business man as I know anywhere. I never yet depended upon him for any thing and found myself disappointed."

"Of course you are bound to stand up for him, since you are his partner," retorted Anne. "No doubt he will show his business capacity by putting all his money into the firm at once. But I suppose there is no help for it. The will is legal, and all that?"

"Perfectly so," replied Mr. Clarendon, calmly. "Mr. Campion was not the man to do such business carelessly. I cannot imagine how he came to leave the addition to his will unsigned."

"I am very glad he did," said Anne. "Kitty is quite trouble enough as it is, without her being left independent of me. I have no doubt that was Mark's doing, and that he expected to be the child's guardian. I remember hearing him talking to John about some such matter, the night John made such a fuss about Kitty's dress. I am heartily glad he is disappointed in his calculation. Well, I must make up my mind to retrench,—to give up my carriage and live in a little house in a back street for the rest of my life. It is very hard, after having been always led to expect something so different; but I suppose I must submit."

"There is no necessity for your making any such sacrifices at present," replied Mr. Clarendon. "You are borrowing trouble at very large interest, my dear madam."

"I think I shall sell this house, at any rate," said Anne. "I shall never think of undertaking all the trouble of housekeeping by myself."

"I would not be in a hurry about that, either. It is much more easy to break up than to settle again; and you will hardly find another home so pleasant and complete as this."

"It will never be pleasant again to me,—never," said Anne, weeping. "Every thing is so changed; and I cannot bear the thought of remaining where I have been so happy. In fact, I made up my mind directly that I should sell this house, even if I should buy another. These rooms are so old-fashioned."

Mr. Clarendon smiled gravely, but made no reply. He had not a high opinion of Mrs. Campion's sense, and he never considered it worth his while to argue with women.

It soon appeared that Anne was quite in earnest about breaking up housekeeping. A purchaser was easily found for the house, which was a very fine one, and desirable in every respect, though rather old-fashioned; and, after casting about for a boarding-place without finding one to suit her, Anne finally decided to go to New York for the winter. Governed by the feeling of jealousy, which had lately increased upon her, she said nothing whatever to Mark and Veronica till the matter was all settled. Mark might have heard of it from Mr. Clarendon, but he had lately been very closely confined at home, making preparations for his new volume. The first news came from Kitty, who did not fancy the changes at all.

"Only think, auntie!" said she, one day, coming into the garden, where Veronica was busy over her bulbs. "Mamma has been and sold our house to Mr. Stanton, and they are going to live in it. Isn't it too bad?"

"Why, Kitty! Has she sold the house?" asked Veronica, in great surprise. "I think that can hardly be. Are you sure?"

"Quite, quite sure," replied Kitty, shaking her head sorrowfully. "I think it is too bad. Mr. and Mrs. Stanton are there now, going all over the house, and talking about making alterations in papa's room, and all," she added, bursting into tears. "I can't bear to have them go into papa's room; and I won't have that ugly Mr. Stanton sit in papa's chair and smoke. I have a great mind to set fire to the house and burn it all down, so that they cannot have it!"

"Hush, hush, Kitty! That is a very wrong way of talking. You would not do any thing so wicked, I am sure."

"I don't care!" cried Kitty, who had worked herself up into one of those frantic fits which Veronica especially dreaded. "He shall not have papa's chair, and mamma is wicked to talk of selling it to him. I told her so, and she only laughed at me, and told me to stay in the nursery; but I wouldn't. I just ran away, and came down here."

"Without asking?" said Rosy, opening her eyes.

"Never mind, Rosy," interposed Veronica. "Kitty, you should not have come without asking; but, now you are here, you may stay and help me, if you will be good and stop crying. Come, now, be quiet at once."

There was something in Veronica's voice which always influenced Kitty, even in her wildest mood. She made a brave effort to check her sobs. Presently Veronica found employment for her and Rosy in carrying away the dried tops of the lilies and portulaccas which she had pulled up; and before long the little girls were laughing gayly over their work and seeing which could carry the biggest basketful. In the midst of the fun, Anne's carriage stopped at the gate, and Anne herself came in. She had never been at the house before since John's death. She looked very pretty and youthful, in her deep and fashionable weeds; and her face was composed to the proper expression of solemnity. Both voice and face changed, however, as she caught sight of Kitty, whose black frock was certainly not improved in appearance by her gardening operations.

"Kitty, you naughty child! How did you come here, and what have you been about? You look like a little beggar-girl!"

"Kitty has been helping me in the garden," said Veronica. "It is only loose dust, Anne, which will easily brush off. I saw that she had on an old frock before I set her to work."

"Not so very old, either. She has only had it three months," said Anne; "though no one could ever guess so to see the state it is in, spotted from top to bottom. You are a pig, Kitty! Why can't you be neat, like Rosy?"

"I don't care," returned Kitty, sullenly. "I can't help it."

"Yes, that is your motto! 'Don't care,' indeed! What do you think your poor papa would say to see you such a naughty girl?"

"Go to Becky, Kitty, and ask her to brush your dress clean and wash your face and hands," interposed Veronica, dreading another outburst from Kitty. "The fault was mine, Anne, I assure you," she added, as the children went away together. "Kitty seemed to feel so unhappy, that I set her to work as the best means of diverting her. She tells me that you have sold your house. Was not that rather a sudden move on your part?"

"No," replied Anne; "not sudden at all. I have been thinking about it ever since Mr. Campion died. With my reduced income, it is necessary for me to be economical."

Anne was fond of talking about her reduced income, and she had repeated the phrase so many times that she really began to believe in it herself.

"Mr. Clarendon told me he did not think any particular economy would be necessary on your part," observed Veronica.

"I wish Mr. Clarendon would not gossip about my affairs," was the reply.

"There was no gossip in the matter," said

Veronica, determined not to be ruffled. "As your nearest relations, I suppose he thought we would be interested to understand your affairs. I hope you get a good price for your house, since you feel obliged to sell it?"

"Eight thousand," said Anne. "Mr. Clarendon seems satisfied; though I really think he might have got more if he had tried."

"And what do you mean to do now?"

"Break up and go to boarding. Indeed, I have pretty much made up my mind to go to New York for the winter. I need a change; and Kitty ought to have better educational advantages than she has here."

"Better educational advantages for a child who can scarcely read!" thought Veronica; but she said nothing, and Anne continued:—

"I shall send her to school,—perhaps to boarding-school. She is growing very troublesome, and needs stricter discipline than my health and spirits are equal to." And Anne heaved a proper and becoming sigh.

"It will come rather hard upon her," Veronica could not help saying. "She has been used to so much liberty all her life."

"She has been used to a great deal too much liberty," replied Anne, fretfully. "Her poor, dear papa always spoiled her so. She carried on so this morning that I was perfectly ashamed of her. I am sure I have done every thing in the world for her; and it is rather hard to have her tell me, before strangers, that she did not love me a bit, as she did before Mr. and Mrs. Stanton to-day."

"I should not allow children to make such speeches," said Veronica, remembering how often Kitty had been allowed to say the same thing unreproved when she was a little child, lest she should be made insincere by restraint. "They do not seem to matter so much when children are young; but they have a different sound at Kitty's age."

"Well, I can't help that now," returned Anne. "She is as she is, and I must make the best of her. I never saw a child alter as she has done during the last two years. It is all the fault of my own good nature in taking Kitty and letting you have Rosy. I never do make a sacrifice but I have reason to repent. However, that is neither here nor there. I came to see if you would like to take some of my furniture in case I sell it."

"Mark would like the furniture of John's room, I know," replied Veronica. "As to the rest, you know we have lately replenished our house so far as was necessary. However, I shall be glad to store any thing for you that you may wish to dispose of in that way. Thanks to our old-fashioned house that you laugh at, we have a spacious garret."

"I thought you would probably buy a new house, now you are so much richer."

"Oh, no. This house suits us perfectly, now that we have the garden and library. When do you mean to break up?"

"I shall begin directly. There is so much to do that I quite dread it, and I want to settle myself before winter. I wish you and Mark would come over this evening and decide upon what things you want. Where is Kitty?"

"She and Rosy are playing in the library. I was going to suggest that she might stay here while you are breaking up. She will be out of your way; and I think she will enjoy the visit."

Anne said she would think of it. Veronica and Mark went over in the evening, according to appointment, and Anne, in a sudden fit of generosity, made them a present of all John's books and furniture, together with some very heavy old chairs and some ancient china, which had gone to him on the family breaking-up, and on which Anne set no value.

Kitty was a little comforted when she learned that Uncle Mark was to have papa's things; but her grief was renewed when she saw the carpets actually torn up and the furniture removed in preparation for the sale. She alternated constantly between passionate bursts of crying and long fits of moping, in which she wandered about the house, turning over and surveying all the familiar objects from which she was soon to be separated. Anne, really touched by her grief, made many efforts to comfort her by extra petting, and by tales of the wonderful and beautiful things she would see in New York; but Kitty steadfastly refused consolation.

"Papa won't be there, nor Uncle Mark, nor any one that I care about," she sobbed, in one of her confidences to Rosy, with whom she was spending her last few days. "It will be all strange and hateful: I know it will."

"But we can write to one another; and how nice that will be!" said Rosy. "Mamma said we might."

"But I can't write," said Kitty.

"You can learn, you know," replied Rosy.

"But can't you write, Kitty? Why, I could write two years ago. I wrote a letter to papa when he was in Boston, direction and all; and mamma said it was a very good letter indeed."

"I am a dunce," said Kitty, despondingly. "Every one says so,—even Uncle Mark. I do every thing that is bad and naughty all the time, and I can't help it. Mamma says she is ashamed of me, because I get my frocks so dirty; and I know I do, but I can't help that either. I don't see how you keep yourself so clean, Rosy."

"I don't know, I am sure, unless it is because I learned when I was little," replied Rosy. "Mamma used to give me a penny for spending-money if I wore my apron two days without a spot."

"That is just it," said Kitty. "I wish I had learned when I was little, and then it would not be so hard. Mamma is always scolding me about something, and then she says, 'Why don't you do like Rosy?' till I feel as if I hated you and her and everybody."

"Oh, Kitty, how can you say so?" exclaimed Rosy, greatly distressed. "How can you say you hate me?"

"I don't hate you," replied Kitty, putting her arms round her sister's neck. "I didn't mean that. I love you dearly: so don't cry, Rosy. But it does make me feel ugly when mamma says such things."

"But you ought to be good, Kitty, and then Aunt Anne would not scold you," said Rosy, whose faith in her own mother's justice was firm as a rock. "If we are naughty, we are found fault with, of course; but not if we are good."

Kitty shook her head. "It don't make much difference, that I see; and, besides, I don't know how to be good. And it is so tiresome to think about it all the time. If I had learned when I was little, then it would be easier; and, besides,—I know something, Rosy, and I will tell you, if you will promise never to tell any one."

"I don't know about that," said Rosy, doubtfully. "I always do tell papa every thing, when he takes me on his knee at night."

"Then I shall not tell you; because Jane told me I must not let any one know."

"Well, never mind," said Rosy. "Let us have one more play with our dolls and dishes.

I will ask Becky to give us some cake and things."

"I don't care much about dolls now; but I will play if you like, Rosy," said Kitty, rather disappointed at Rosy's want of curiosity. But her mind was quite too full of her secret to keep it to herself, and out it came at last.

"Only think, Rosy! Jane says I am not mamma's own child, and you are not your mamma's, either. She says our own mamma died in the hospital,—just think, Rosy! in the hospital, where the poor people go!—and that your mamma and mine adopted us, and that our mamma was poor. And Jane says," she continued, bursting into tears, "that people always get tired of adopted children after a while, and that mamma is tired of me, and that is the reason she scolds me so."

"Then Jane is a wicked woman to say such things, and you are a naughty, wicked child to listen to her!" said Rosy, with indignant decision. "I don't believe one word of it."

"It is true, for all that," returned Kitty. "Jane says she lived at our house when mamma brought me home, and that I had hardly any clothes at all till she dressed me, and that I was a year old then. And she says we are twins, and that our own papa was a bad man, and did not treat our own mamma well, and that was what killed her. So papa was not my own father, after all."

Rosy looked perfectly stunned at the intelligence which came upon her. "Then I am not my mamma's child, either, nor papa's! I am an orphan, like the little children at the Home! Oh, papa, papa! Oh, what shall I do?" And Rosy threw herself down upon the sofa, in an agony of crying and sobbing very unusual with her.

Kitty, much alarmed at the effect of her words, tried in vain to quiet her; and at last Becky came in.

"Why, what is the matter, children?" she exclaimed. "What are you crying about?"

"We are crying because I am going away to-morrow," replied Kitty, to whom a false excuse was no novelty. Rosy was silent.

"Poor dears!" said Becky; "no wonder you feel badly about it; but don't cry. That won't do any good. Winter will be gone before you know it; and just think of all the things you will have to tell each other in the spring. Come, I am going to make some nice cake, and you shall help me. I am going to make each of you a bird's-nest cake. I bought the almonds and citron on purpose this very morning."

But not even the honour of grating nutmegs and blanching almonds,—not even the frosted cake crowned with a bird's nest of sliced citrons, containing four sugar-almond eggs,—not Anne's parting present of the long-coveted and beautifully-furnished little writing-desk,—could lift the weight from Rosy's spirits. Her father and mother noticed her depression, but naturally attributed it to grief at parting with Kitty; and Rosy did not undeceive them. For the first time she dreaded the evening hour with her father,—for the first time went to bed with a secret on her mind and a weight on her conscience!

CHAPTER X.

ROSY'S SECRET.

THE day passed on, and still Rosy was depressed, losing her interest in all her employments, caring neither to work nor play, unwilling to be a minute away from father and mother, but silent and reserved in their company. Veronica became seriously alarmed, especially as the child's health seemed to be failing.

"Come, Rosy," said she, one afternoon, "I want you to go round to the 'Home' for me. I want to send Miss Brown the yarn I bought for her yesterday, and Mrs. Norris has some new kittens which you have never seen."

Rosy had always looked upon a visit to the "Home" as one of her great treats. The old ladies were all very fond of her, and sometimes almost quarrelled as to who should have her to tea; and she was happy in the little services she was able to render them,—in dusting Miss Brown's books, and arranging Mrs. Olin's basket, and watching Mrs. Holloway make lace on the lace-pillow she had brought from Devonshire so long ago. But to-day she hung back.

"Can't Nelly carry the yarn?" she asked.

"Nelly is busy; and, besides, I want you to go. The walk will do you good, and it would not be kind to Mrs. Norris to refuse her invitation. Come, find your hat and basket, and gather a bunch of rosemary and bergamot for Mrs. Grimes, the blind woman."

The habit of unquestioning obedience prevailed, and Rosy set out on her mission; but it was with such evident reluctance to leave home, even for an hour, that Veronica did not know what to think of her.

"I cannot understand all this grief for Kitty, unless there is something in the old notion of a peculiarly close tie between twins," said she to Mark, who had been listening to the conversation. "I never thought Kitty and Rosy were particularly congenial."

"There is something more about it," said Mark. "The child has a weight upon her spirits. I should almost think some one had been frightening her."

"Who could possibly frighten her?"

"She has something upon her mind, more than Kitty's going away," said Mark. "I have been watching her for some days, and I am sure of it. I must try and find out what the matter is."

"Can you give any guess?" asked Veronica.

"I am quite sure the trouble dates from Kitty's last day's visit. Is it possible that Kitty can have led her into any scrape?"

"It is just possible. Kitty has grown sly lately. She may have done something wrong and made Rosy promise not to tell. We have taught her to be so truthful that a hastily extorted promise may be weighing upon her. I will try to find out this evening."

Rosy came home from her visit somewhat enlivened. Mrs. Norris was going to save the prettiest kitten for her. She had taken up the stitches upon Mrs. Grimes's knitting, and had read her library-book all through to her and Miss Brown. She drank tea with Mrs. Norris, and washed up the tea-things afterwards, and watered all her flowers, and Granny Pratt's as well. All these labours of love cheered her for a time; but the depression returned in full force.

Poor Rosy! She was indeed to be pitied. The solid ground on which she had walked all her life, seemed to have been cut away by Kitty's communication, and she felt as though she had nothing to which she could trust. The more she thought, the more reason she saw to believe Kitty's tale. It explained many little things which had puzzled her,—remarks she had overheard among the old ladies and from visitors, and speeches of Aunt Anne's to Kitty when she was displeased,—especially one overheard by her on the occasion of Anne's last visit:—"You may thank your good luck that I gave up Rosy to you and took Kitty myself." Was it really true that parents did tire of adopted children? Would there come a time when mamma would feel about her as Aunt Anne did about Kitty?

But there was something more resting upon Rosy's mind than the discovery she had made. She felt that she had agreed to Kitty's falsehood by allowing Becky to believe that they were crying for their approaching separation, and that she was deceiving her parents by permitting them to think she was grieving for her sister. More than once she had made up her mind to tell papa all; but, then, papa so hated any thing like a lie,—would not such a confession hasten the day she dreaded, when he and mamma would begin to look coldly upon her and turn her off?—and, then, what would Kitty think?

It was a terrible strait for the strong feelings and sensitive conscience of the little one; and well it was for her that she had a wise friend to deal with her. When Mark took her on his knee in the fire-lighted library that night, he held her silently against his breast for some minutes, while his heart was lifted up to the Fountain of Wisdom, that he might have discretion and grace given him to deal with the child of his love.

"It seems to me," he said, at last, tenderly, "that my little Rosy has some secret trouble on her mind, which she has been hiding from papa and mamma. Is it not so, my love?"

Rosy breathed a sigh, which was almost a sob, and nestled closer, but she made no reply.

"Has any one been frightening you, Rosy?"

"No, papa,—not frightening, exactly,—but——"

"But what, sweetheart? Tell papa all about it."

Rosy could no longer refrain. She clasped her arms round her father's neck, and sobbed out, "Oh, papa, it isn't true, is it?"

"What is not true, love?"

"What Kitty says,—what Jane told Kitty,—that you and mamma are not my own papa and mamma,—that my real papa and mamma are dead. Oh, papa! papa!" And, lifting her head and seeming to read in her father's face the confirmation of her fears, she dropped it again on his shoulder, and sobbed bitterly, with those deep drawn-sobs which are so heart-rending in a little child.

Mark drew a long breath. It had come, then,—the time he had always dreaded and had never been able to make up his mind how to meet. He clasped Rosy still closer, and bent his face upon her glossy curls for a few minutes.

"Rosy, my dearest child, listen to me," he said, in that tender, calm voice peculiarly his own. "I meant to tell you all this myself, and perhaps I have been to blame in not doing so before, instead of leaving you to hear it from strangers. Quiet yourself now, and listen, and I will tell you the whole story."

Rosy made a brave effort, and by degrees the

sobs ceased, though she did not lift up her head.

"It is true, my dear, that in one way you are not our own child,—not as Nelly is her mother's own child. Your mother was a dear friend of mamma's, who died here on her way to New England. Your father died before you and Kitty were born; and when your mother found that she was going to heaven, she gave you to mamma for her own child as long as you should live. You are as much ours as Nelly is her mother's, but in a different way."

"Then my own mother was not a poor woman?" said Rosy. "Jane told Kitty that she was, and that was the reason she was in the hospital; and she said my father was a bad, wicked man, and abused her."

"I will tell you all the circumstances, so far as I know them, Rosy, and you can judge for yourself." He then went over the outlines of Daisy's history, and added, in conclusion, "I believe it is true that your father did many wrong things during his lifetime. He was not brought up to love God and try to please him, as you have been. But he repented of all his sins before his death, and I have not the least doubt that God forgave him and that he is now happy with your mother in heaven. It is not true that he ever ill treated her. She told me herself that he was never any thing but perfectly kind to her."

"Oh, I am so glad!" said Rosy. "It seemed so dreadful that he should have been wicked and died——" Rosy stopped, but Mark well understood what she had been thinking of.

"But Jane says," continued Rosy, "that people who adopt children——" Rosy stopped short. She was already beginning to be ashamed of her fears.

"Well?" said Mark, who guessed what was coming. "Perhaps she said that people who adopt children always tire of them, and ill treat them after a while. Did she?"

"Yes, papa."

"And did my Rosy think that her papa and mamma, who have taken care of her all her life, would treat her so cruelly?" asked Mark, tenderly, but with a look and tone which went straight to Rosy's heart. "What have they ever done, that their little daughter should think so hardly of them?"

"Oh, papa, don't!" cried Rosy. "Oh, I am so sorry and so ashamed! Please do forgive me, papa."

"I forgive you, my daughter, and I hope you will never be so foolish again. Suppose, because some people say that adopted children always turn out badly, we should begin to watch you to see whether you were not going to be ungrateful and undutiful?"

"Why do people say such things, papa?"

"I suppose it comes about in this way. People who adopt children often begin by indulging them in every thing, letting them have their own way, and spoiling them, as we say. This makes the children troublesome, selfish, and disagreeable. When they grow older, their faults show more plainly and become more annoying and hard to bear with. The children are selfish and exacting, and the parents lose patience with the very faults they have helped to make. The same thing often happens with parents and their own children."

"I know when we were up at Clifton, summer before last, Aunt Anne did not think Kitty could do any thing wrong," remarked Rosy. "She always thought it was my fault, or somebody's, whenever Kitty quarrelled with the other children. But Kitty used to mind Uncle John; and I think she loved him a great deal more than Aunt Anne."

"There is another thing, Rosy, that you may learn," continued Mark. "Do you think it is very pleasant to have a secret?"

"No, indeed!" said Rosy, heartily. "I never want to have another as long as I live. I think it is dreadful."

"Then remember this, my dear: whenever any one wishes you to have a secret from your father and mother, be sure they are wrong. We want you to feel that we are your best friends, and more interested in giving you pleasure than any one else can be. So I hope you will have no more concealments,—unless, indeed, you should wish to surprise me with a fine new pair of slippers for a Christmas-present," he added, smiling. "In that case I permit you to keep your design a secret till the time comes."

"I think Kitty loves to have secrets," remarked Rosy. "She very often says, 'Now, don't you ever tell,' when it is of no consequence at all. And I know she and Jane have secrets from Aunt Anne."

"What sort of secrets?"

"Well, Jane's cousin keeps an ice-cream saloon over the river. Jane often takes Kitty there, and they give her ice-cream and candy;

but Jane always says, 'Now, mind, Miss Kitty, you don't tell mamma.'"

"That is very wrong in Jane," said Mark. "It is teaching the child to deceive her mother."

"Papa, where was my other mamma buried?" asked Rosy, after a little pause.

"Do you remember that long grave at Mount Faith, by the side of little brother and sisters, where mamma told you to plant the violets? That is Mamma Daisy's grave. I intend to put up a cross for her, but I have been waiting till you should be old enough to understand. Now I will have it done directly, and you shall go with me to choose the marble."

"And papa, please, will you take my gold pieces which Uncle John gave me on my birthday, to pay for it? I have never spent one of them; and I should so like to do something for dear Mamma Daisy. Will you, please, papa?"

"Yes, my love, if you wish. And, now, is your heart at ease?"

"Yes, papa."

"And you will not be so foolish as to think papa and mamma are growing tired of you, even if they do find fault with you sometimes?"

"No, papa. I never should have thought of such a thing, only for Kitty. I am sure mamma never scolded me so much in all my life as Mrs. Wicks scolds Nelly in one day."

And so this great matter was settled, and Rosy's mind relieved of its burden. The trouble threatened to come back when, in the course of two or three months, a little brother was born. At first nothing could exceed Rosy's joy; but her pleasure was somewhat damped by a very innocent speech from Nelly Wicks.

"Are you not sorry you have got a little brother, Rosy?"

"Why, no!" exclaimed Rosy, indignantly. "I am as glad as I can be."

"But your mother will not love you any more, now she has got a younger one," said Nelly. "My ma loved me dearly till Molly came. She used to give me every thing, and pet and kiss me; but she has never loved me since. And she did just so by Alick when I was born, I know; for he said so."

"Your mother might do so, but I don't believe my mother will," said Rosy, with an instinctive sense of the difference. Nevertheless, she was not without her apprehensions for a while, till she found that she was as much petted as ever, and even more so by Becky, who was also not without her fears that her nursling's rights would be encroached upon by the new-comer.

In the course of the winter, Mark went to New York on business about his forthcoming book. He called to see Anne, whom he found established in a fashionable boarding-house, with a circle of fine acquaintances about her, and ready to wonder how she could ever have endured life in such a dull place as Milby. Kitty was at a fashionable French school as day-boarder, and Mark heard great accounts of her progress and improvement; though Anne admitted that she saw very little of the child except upon Saturdays. The next day being a holiday, Mark asked and obtained permission to take Kitty out with him for a whole long morning. Kitty was overjoyed. She certainly was greatly improved in outward manners, and was learning to take a little care of her dress, and to keep her hands and teeth clean; but she was thinner than ever, and the shy, sullen look she had begun to wear was painfully apparent when she was left to herself. Once alone with Uncle Mark, all her troubles were poured out in a flood. The school was hateful, the girls detestable; she could not understand her lessons or learn them; she was scolded all the time, mamma **was** very unkind, and nobody loved her, and she wished she was dead and buried. Mark soothed and sympathized, and tried to come at the truth; but this was not easy. Kitty could not see that she was at all to blame for any of her troubles. She was forced to admit that she was often cross and passionate, but she thought it was all mamma's fault for not teaching her better when she was little. In short, while she had the liveliest notion of her own rights, she had no conception of the duties she owed to others. She was to have every thing done for her, and not to give any thing in return. All her troubles were charged on the fact of her being an adopted child, and she thought if she only had her own dear mamma she should be perfectly happy.

"If you had your own mamma, you would be obliged to obey her," said Mark. "She taught you to mind her when you were only a baby."

"I should not mind obeying her," said Kitty. "She would have a right to make me."

"And has not your mamma a right to make you? What would have become of you if she had not taken you? You must have gone to the orphan-asylum."

This was a new idea to Kitty.

"Would not you have taken me, Uncle Mark?"

"No, my dear: I could not have afforded it. I was poor then, and had to work hard even to support Aunt Veronica and Rosy. And moreover, Kitty, we should never have known of your existence but for your mamma. It was she who found you in the hospital, and she came at once to tell Aunt Veronica. She took you home when you were a little baby, unable to do the least thing for yourself or any one, and she has taken care of and supported you ever since. How are you going to repay her for all the care and expense you have caused her these eight or nine years?"

It was a new and not an agreeable notion to Kitty that she was the one indebted, and not her mother. She renewed her complaints of school, schoolmates, and every one else.

"I will tell you where a great part of your trouble lies, Kitty," said Mark, interrupting the catalogue of grievances. "It is because you are all the time seeking to please yourself,—a thing which people seldom succeed in doing. You think the girls ought to make themselves agreeable to you; but you do not seem to remember that you ought also to make yourself agreeable to them. You complain of Madame, but I don't find, from what you say, that you have really any thing to find fault with."

"She says I don't try to learn my lessons," interrupted Kitty.

"And do you?"

"Sometimes I do; but they are so hard."

"Then you must try all the harder: that is all. When mamma finds fault, don't think, 'If she were my own mamma she would not do so,' but say to yourself, 'Mamma has brought me up and taken care of me when I had no other friend, and I ought to try and please her,' and endeavour to do better next time. And, Kitty, above all, remember that you have a Father in heaven who loves you and whom you must try to please. Do you say your prayers?"

"Sometimes, when I don't forget," said Kitty, hanging her head.

"But you must not forget. Suppose God should forget to take care of you,—to give you air to breathe, and light to see by, and friends to care for you. You cannot be happy while you forget your Father in heaven; but if you try to please him and ask him to help you to be good, you will find that he will make your way easy to you, and assist you in winning the love of those about you."

It was a new idea to Kitty that she was to win love and favour by her own exertions; but she promised to try. Mark felt very sorry for the poor child, and almost wished to take her home with him, at least for a visit; but Anne would not hear of it. The child was just coming under some sort of discipline, and she could not have her all broken up again. Mark ventured to hint that it might be well for Kitty to learn some other things before beginning French and music; but here again Anne had a theory. Kitty must begin French young, or she would never learn the true accent. She only wished she had taught her to read French in the first place, even before she learned her English letters. She had requested Madame to let the child have all her lessons in that language; but Madame said she would have to learn a little more of it first. Mark said no more, thankful at least to find that the schoolmistress had some sense. Anne was graciousness itself to Mark, and would willingly have made a great lion of him; but he was not to be lionized, and she was fain to content herself with talking about him instead of showing him off.

She sent a handsome present to the baby, and Kitty loaded him with gifts for Aunt Veronica, little Johnny, and Rosy. Her last words were, "Tell Rosy I hate New York just as much as I said I should."

CHAPTER XI.

AN UNWELCOME VISITOR.

ONE afternoon in the latter part of summer, Rosy was left quite alone in the house. Mark and Veronica were out, driving with baby, and Rebecca had stepped over to see poor Mrs. Wicks, whose health had been for some time declining. Rosy was not at all afraid of being left alone: in fact, she rather enjoyed having the house to herself, and she was never lonely so long as she had her doll, her books, and the cat, for company. The little girl was sitting in the bay window of the back parlour, when she saw a carriage, freighted with two or three trunks, draw up to the door. Rosy's only thought was of Aunt Anne and Kitty, and, full of joy, she ran to meet the welcome guests and do the honours of the house. She was disappointed. A tall, stout, middle-aged lady, whom Rosy had never seen before, descended from the carriage.

"Is this Mark Campion's house?" she asked, sharply.

The tone rather grated upon Rosy's ears; but she answered, politely,—

"Yes, ma'am; but papa and mamma are not at home."

"Humph!" said the visitor, looking at her keenly. "What's your name, child?"

"Rosa Brush Campion," was the reply; "but papa and mamma call me Rosy."

"Humph!" said the visitor, again. "And when will your mamma, as you call her, be at home?"

"She will be at home soon," replied Rosy, very much perplexed; but, remembering her good manners,—" Won't you come in and stay till she comes?"

"Of course I shall. I have come to stay. Take off the trunks," added the stranger, turning to the hackman; "and you, child, call a servant and have them taken up-stairs."

"We have no servant but Becky, and she is not at home; but the trunks can stand on the veranda till mamma comes," said Rosy. "Please walk in, ma'am."

The stranger followed Rosy into the back parlour, and seated herself in Mark's favourite chair.

"Come here to me, child," said she, taking both her hands and gazing fixedly at her. "What did you say your name was?"

Rosy repeated her name again.

"Nonsense!" said the visitor. "Your name is Rosa Brush, and nothing else. Did no one ever tell you so before?"

"I know that my dear Mamma Daisy's name was Brush," said Rosy, beginning to wish very much that some one would come. "It is on the cross which papa put up over her grave at Mount Faith:—'Daisy Brush, aged twenty-four.'"

"So you do know something of the matter. Did no one ever tell you about your aunt Adela?"

"No, ma'am: I never heard of her," said Rosy; and, indeed, Mark had never thought it necessary to make her aware of her aunt's existence. "I did not know I had any aunt but Aunt Anne."

"You have no aunt but Aunt Adela: understand that," said Miss Brush. "I am your only relation, so far as I know, unless your mother had some cousins. You belong to me, and to no one else."

"I belong to papa and mamma," said Rosy, indignantly. "My own dear Mamma Daisy gave me to them when I was a little bit of a baby, just before she died. Papa told me so himself, and he said I was his very own, to keep forever!"

Miss Brush laughed sarcastically. "We shall soon see," said she, releasing the hands by which she had held Rosy close to her side. "There is no particular use in debating the matter with *you*. I have made up my own mind, and that is enough. Who is this coming in?"

"It is mamma," said Rosy, experiencing a sensation of intense relief; for she had been considerably scared by her aunt's words and manner, and, in her alarm, began to think it possible that she might be carried off by force before her mother's return. "I will tell her that you are here."

She brought such an agitated face to the door that Veronica was startled.

"What is the matter, my darling? Has any thing frightened you?"

"No, mamma,—yes, mamma, a little!—

Have I really got an aunt Adela? There is a lady here who says she is my aunt Adela, and that I belong to her. I don't: do I?"

"No, my love. You belong to no one but me," replied Veronica. "No one shall ever take you from me: so do not be frightened. Where is Aunt Adela?"

"She is in the parlour, and she has brought her trunks; and Rebecca was not at home; and—oh, mamma, was it silly?—I could not help being frightened!"

"I don't wonder," said Veronica. "Come into the nursery, Rosy. I will just lay baby down, and then go to see Aunt Adela. She is your father's sister, Rosy, and we must be civil to her while she stays; though I must say she is the last person I ever expected to see here."

Veronica might have said with truth what she came near saying,—that Miss Brush was the last person she wished to see. It was easy to guess that she had come with the intention of possessing herself of one, perhaps both, of the children; and Veronica foresaw a great deal of annoyance to all the persons concerned. But she could not be uncivil in her own house. She welcomed her old schoolmate with tolerable cordiality, installed her in a pleasant bedroom up-stairs, and went to consult with Becky about the dinner. Becky had already heard from Rosy of the new arrival, and was prepared to do battle on the instant.

"A pretty business, to be sure, coming and taking possession of people's houses in that way! I only wish I had been at home! I would have given her a good lesson."

"On the whole, perhaps, it is as well that you were not," said Veronica, smiling. "But, now that Miss Brush is here, Becky, we must be civil to her as long as she stays. I have been thinking we had better borrow Nelly Wicks for a few days to help about the house. I dare say Miss Brush has been used to a good deal of attention."

"I suppose when she comes to see us she can live as we do," said Becky, who had made up her mind to uncompromising hostility. "However, I have no objection to calling in Nelly for a while. It will be a change for her; and she needs one,—poor thing!"

Miss Brush came down when dinner was ready, elegantly dressed, and with an evident determination to overawe the whole household. She did not succeed, however. Mark's gentle, unassuming dignity, and Veronica's even composure, were not in the least disturbed by her grand airs, and even Rosy had recovered from her fright, and chatted away merrily to her father and mother. Old Nero, now the most ancient of all the cats, assumed his usual place at Mark's right hand, and begged for morsels of bread, unawed by the close vicinity of Miss Brush's rustling brocade. Miss Brush seemed to expect to carry all before her without opposition, and already began to treat Rosy as though she belonged to her; and, as the child was relating to her father some new exploit of baby's, she checked her sharply with,—

"There! that will do, Rose! Be quiet. Little girls should be seen, and not heard."

Rosy looked up in innocent confusion, and Veronica's face flushed with indignation, but Mark evinced no discomposure. He opened his eyes upon Miss Brush with an expression of well-bred surprise, and then, turning to Rosy, asked, "What were you saying, daughter?"

Something of mischief sparkled in Rosy's eyes as she finished her tale, and Miss Brush was irritated accordingly.

"In my day, children were taught to be silent before their elders," said she.

"Rosy has been taught not to interrupt the

conversation of others, whether elders or juniors," said Mark, politely. "She has been the only child a long time, however; and she has always been permitted to talk very freely to papa and mamma."

"She has been very sufficiently spoiled, I dare say," returned Miss Brush. "Her mother was a spoiled child before her. However, there is time enough to correct all that."

Mark shrugged his shoulders and elevated his eyebrows, but made no other reply. Coffee was presently brought in, accompanied by some dainty cakes, and Rosy was helped with the rest. Miss Brush looked disapprovingly at her portion.

"When you live with me, miss, you will have no such rich cake as that, I can tell you," said she. "Cake is not fit for children."

"If Rosy should ever come to visit you, Miss Brush, I dare say she will be governed by your rules, as she is now by mine," said Veronica, with a decided emphasis upon the word *visit;* "but I am afraid it will be a long time before I spare her even to make a visit so far away from home."

Miss Brush tossed her head and made no reply. After dinner was over in the kitchen,

Mark called his household together, as usual, for prayers. He had begun the custom of early evening prayers at the time when he was obliged to remain late at the office, and it had been continued upon Rosy's account. Rosy, who imitated in every thing her father's gracious politeness, offered her aunt a book; but Miss Brush declined, and sat by in disdainful indifference, taking particular pains to look out of the window all the time Mark was reading, and sitting bolt upright through the prayer. Presently Mark returned to the library, and Rosy followed him for that precious twilight hour of talk which neither of them ever willingly missed. Miss Brush, who seemed bent upon making herself as disagreeable as possible, rose to follow them. This was a little more than Veronica could stand; and she interposed:—

"Excuse me, Miss Brush, but I think my husband would prefer not to be interrupted at present. He always gives an hour in the evening to our daughter's religious instruction."

"Humph!" said Miss Brush, returning to her seat, however. "So you have married a man as methodistical as yourself, Veronica! I remember you used to set up for a saint at school. I did not expect to find Mark Campion one of that sort."

"I don't know how any one who reads his books could expect to find him any thing else," said Veronica. "He is not always dragging in sacred names and Scripture phrases, but I am sure no books were ever more pervaded with the spirit of true godliness."

"Stuff and nonsense!" returned Miss Brush. "I suppose he writes what he thinks will suit the market, like other people; but it is useless to tell me that a man of his mind and cultivation believes in all those antiquated myths. I know better."

Veronica could not quite trust her voice with a reply. Miss Brush continued:—"I suppose we may as well have our talk out now as any other time. Of course you know that I have come for that child. It has not been convenient for me to take her before: so I have been content to leave her with you, especially as I hate babies. But, now that she has arrived at a convenient age, I intend to take her to live with me, repaying, of course, all expenses which you have incurred thus far. You can make out your account to suit yourself. I shall not dispute it, unless it should be out of all reason exorbitant. I suppose you will be willing enough to get rid of her, now that you have a child of your own."

"You are mistaken, Miss Brush," said Veronica, recovering at once her voice and her composure. "Rosy was given to us by her dying mother, and we shall never resign her to any one."

"I am sorry the child is so like her mother," continued Miss Brush, quite disregarding Veronica's words. "I can see the same spirit coming out all over her; and no doubt it has been aggravated by the spoiling she has received. However, I think I can find means to correct that. I propose to set out the day after to-morrow; and I presume you can have her ready by that time."

"Miss Brush, listen to me," said Veronica, firmly. "Once for all, you may lay aside all thought of taking Rosy away with you. She is our child, and ours she shall remain."

"You talk like a fool, Veronica!" said Miss Brush. "What is the child to you?"

"She is every thing to me," replied Veronica. "If she were my own flesh and blood, she could not be dearer. I would as soon give you my baby as Rosy."

The Twin Roses.

"She is our child, and ours she shall remain."   p. 224.

"But do you not see that I have every right to the child? Is she not my only brother's daughter,—the last of my race?"

"If you wanted the child, why did you not keep her when you had her?" asked Veronica. "Why did you make your only brother's widow miserable, and then turn her out of doors to shift for herself?"

Miss Brush winced a little. "I see the artful little fool has told you her own version of the story," said she, recovering herself. "I presume she did not mention that her own light conduct was the cause of her husband's death?"

"She told me that you said so."

"But you did not believe it?"

"No," replied Veronica. "I never knew Daisy to be any thing but truthful; and I do not believe she told me a falsehood upon her dying bed."

"No doubt she made out a fine romantic story of persecution for 'righteousness' sake,'" said Miss Brush. "Perhaps I might have been hard upon her; but she made me sick with her airs, and, above all, with her piety. I know she made people think her a martyr and me a demon. But that does not matter. I shall talk to your husband, Veronica, and I have no

P

doubt I shall convince him of the justice of my claim. If I do so, of course you will give the matter up; and, meantime, I beg you will not prejudice the child against me by any 'raw-head and bloody-bones' stories. If you will give me a candle, I will go to my room; for I feel rather tired."

Veronica was only too glad to get rid of her unwelcome visitor. She provided light, saw that the room was made comfortable, and then returned to the library, where she found Rosy still nestled in her father's arms.

"Well," said Mark, "has the dragon gone to roost? Here is Rosy afraid that she is going to be carried off, like another lovely Sabra, with no champion to defend her."

"The dragon has retired for the night, I hope," replied Veronica. "I never saw any one more altered,—in manner, I mean; for I can see that she is the same at heart. She used to be 'smoother than butter,' gaining all her ends by management and diplomacy; but she seems to think now that she has nothing to do but to drive straight on over everybody."

"She has had fifteen years of arbitrary power since you knew her," remarked her husband. "What wind blew her here?"

"The wind of her own fancy, I presume."

"Mamma, do you think that Aunt Adela has come for me?" asked Rosy, anxiously.

"I presume she has, my dear; but you need not be frightened. Papa and I have no notion of letting you go."

"No, indeed," said Mark. "Our little Rosy has grown in our garden too long to be transplanted. Do not let your heart be troubled by any such fear."

"Well, I *was* frightened!" said Rosy, candidly. "She looked so tall and big, and she held my hand so tight when she said, 'You belong to me and to no one else.' Oh, how I did wish some one would come!"

"I do not wonder," said Mark. "But you may sleep in peace, my daughter. No one but God shall ever take you from us. Goodnight." But Rosy still lingered. "Well, what is it now?"

"Please, mamma, may I ask Becky to let me sleep with her to-night?"

Veronica smiled. "Yes, certainly, my love. Poor child!" she added, as Rosy closed the door. "No wonder she is afraid to sleep alone."

CHAPTER XII.

A CONTEST.

MISS BRUSH came down to breakfast, apparently in a somewhat more amiable mood. She was particularly gracious to Rosy, who, relieved by her faith in her father's assurance that no one should take her from him, responded in the pretty, cordial manner natural to her, and readily brought her books and her work to show how much she had learned.

"You seem to have done very well, so far," said Miss Brush. "I suppose you have not begun French yet?"

"She has been waiting to learn a little more English first," said Veronica.

"My maid speaks the language very well," said Miss Brush. "I intend she shall give the child lessons, as French is so much spoken in our set. My mother's family were French, and, though she married an American, we have always kept about the same circle of acquaintance. I presume Rose will acquire it easily enough. What do you say, Rose? Will you come to New Orleans with me, and be my little girl?"

"I am papa's and mamma's little girl," said Rosy. "I cannot belong to any one else. Papa would not know what to do without me:—would you, papa?"

"No, my dear. I should feel lost indeed without my little daughter," replied Mark.

"But he is not your own papa, Rosy," said Miss Brush, with a darkening brow, but plainly putting a great constraint upon herself. "Mr. and Mrs. Campion are not in the least related to you, while I am your own aunt,—your own father's sister; and you were born in my house."

"Was I?" asked Rosy, innocently. "Why didn't you keep me in your house, then, Aunt Adela?" Miss Brush's eyes shot fire; but Rosy continued, unconscious of offence:—"I was in the hospital when mamma found me:—wasn't I, mamma? We went up and saw the Sister that used to take care of Mamma Daisy, and I carried her some flowers from my garden.

She is such a nice woman, Aunt Adela, only she wears such a funny thing on her head."

"But, Rosy, if you come and live with me you will be very rich," continued Miss Brush. "You will have a fine carriage and horses, and a pony, perhaps, and a maid of your own to dress you every day."

"I can dress myself," said Rosy, rather indignantly. "I have dressed myself this whole year,—ever since little brother was born. My papa is rich enough to get me all I want; and, if he wasn't, I would never go away from him and mamma,—not if they were as poor as old Aunt Phebe,—never!"

"Listen to me, Rose," said Miss Brush, sharply. "You belong to me, and I intend to have you, at all events. If you come with a good grace, so much the better for you. I shall not promise to spoil you, as these people have done, but I shall educate you properly; and if you give me satisfaction, I shall provide for you at my death. Now, be reasonable: forget that you have any other friends, and make up your mind to come with me. It will be better for all parties that intercourse should cease, at least for some years," she continued, speaking to Mark. "I wish the child to forget that she has ever been any thing else but a Southerner."

Rosy took refuge between her father's knees; and the temper natural to her as to Kitty, but rarely seen of late years, flashed out.

"I am not your little girl, and I will never go with you!" she exclaimed. "I love papa and mamma, and I belong to them. Dear Mamma Daisy gave me to them; and I will never go away from them, with you or anybody,—not if I were to have all the carriages and all the money in the world."

"Very well, miss," said Miss Brush, growing pale with rage. "You do credit to your *religious instruction*, I must say. I shall find means to tame that temper of yours before many days, I promise you. Mr. Campion, do you intend to give me possession of my brother's child peaceably, or must I take legal means to recover my rights?"

"Go to Rebecca, my dear," said Mark, speaking to Rosy. "I will go with you." He left the room for a few minutes, and presently returned without the child. "Now, to reply to your questions once for all, as you say, Miss Brush," said he, seating himself deliberately.

"Well?" returned the lady, sharply.

"Well," said Mark, "I do not intend to give you possession of your brother's child, either peaceably or in any other way. We adopted her for our own, at a time when she had no better prospect before her than an almshouse or an orphan-asylum. If you ever had any moral right, you have forfeited it by your long neglect; and as to legal right, you have none whatever. I have taken care of that."

"What do you mean, sir?"

"I mean," returned Mark, with extra deliberation, "that, foreseeing some such difficulty as that which has arisen, at the time we adopted Rosy I caused writings to be drawn up, by which the custody of the child was secured to me. Rosy is regularly apprenticed to me till the age of twenty-one years. The indenture is signed by her mother, and witnessed by the clergyman and physician who attended her during her illness. So, you see, your claim of relationship goes for nothing."

Miss Brush was speechless with rage.

"Moreover, I must tell you another thing," continued Mark, "the knowledge of which I would gladly have spared you if you had been a little more reasonable. At Daisy's request, both my wife and myself pledged ourselves, in the most solemn manner, that, whatever became of Rose, she should never, on any pretext whatever, be put into your hands; and she gave as a reason for requiring this pledge your cruel treatment of her while she was under your roof and dependent upon you. So, you see, we are doubly bound."

"Mighty well, sir," said Miss Brush, finding her voice; "but if you think you are going to turn me from my purpose by any such trick, you are mistaken. I shall have legal advice on the matter."

"Very well, madam. You can do so; but I warn you that you will gain nothing except a bill of costs."

"Where is the child? I demand to see her alone."

"She has gone out for the day," said Veronica. "I preferred having her out of hearing." And, indeed, Becky had taken Rosy round to the Old Ladies' Home, and left her under Miss Brown's guardianship, with a strict injunction not to stir out of doors.

"I suppose you call that a lady-like proceeding?"

"Perfectly," returned Veronica, calmly.

Miss Brush took two or three turns across

the room. She was evidently considerably nonplussed.

"See here," said she, finally. "I don't know why I should take so much pains about this matter, but I am not used to be defeated when I once take a project in hand. Give me this child quietly, without more ado, and I will pay you down five thousand dollars."

Mark's eye began to kindle dangerously. "It is a large sum to pay;—much more than you could get."

"What do you mean?" asked Miss Brush. "You do not suppose I intend to sell the child?"

"As you seem to expect me to sell her, I see nothing unreasonable in the supposition," replied Mark. "But you may dismiss all thought of such a speculation. Rosy is not in the market."

"Well, I have learned something," said Miss Brush. "I always supposed some men would sell any thing."

"You may possibly learn something else," said Mark, erecting his tall figure; "and that is, that there are some insults which a man will not endure even from a woman. I should be sorry to order you out of my house; but——"

"You may save yourself the trouble, Mark Campion," returned Miss Brush, also rising. "I shall leave your house as soon as possible; but it will be to seek a legal remedy. I do not propose to give up so easily. Where is the child?"

"I do not see, exactly, how that is any concern of yours, madam."

"I wish to see her again."

"I see nothing which would be gained by another interview. She has been made sufficiently uncomfortable already. I do not wish her nerves to be further tried. Come, Miss Brush, be reasonable. I can sympathize so far in your disappointment as to make great allowances for you; but what you ask is as entirely out of the question as if you had asked me for a piece of my own heart. Be advised: give up your present plan, seek out some orphan or destitute girl, and make a happy home for her——"

"I want none of your preaching. Am I to see the child again, or not?"

"Not at present," said Mark.

"Very well. I shall say no more: only, you may rest assured of one thing, you have not done Rose any good. She will be none the better off with me for the way in which you have treated me and taught her to regard me: I can tell you that."

Mark made no reply.

"Be so good as to send your servant for a carriage," continued Miss Brush, with freezing loftiness of manner, "and inform me what I am to pay for my board and lodging."

"I will send in the bill as soon as I have time to make it out," replied Mark, relapsing into his usual manner. "My love, will you send Nelly for a carriage?"

The carriage was brought, and Miss Brush departed, shaking off the dust from her feet. She lost no time in fulfilling her threat of seeking legal advice. Fortunately for her, the lawyer to whom she went was an honest man, and above making business for himself. He looked at the papers, and talked with Rosy herself alone, and ended by assuring Miss Brush that she had no remedy.

"If the child was unhappy or ill treated, or if she wished herself to go with you, something might perhaps be done; but she is so clearly well off, and manifests such a degree of fear and horror at the very thought of going away with you, that I see nothing but to let her stay where she is, unless Mr. Campion can be persuaded to forego his claim."

"That I shall never do," said Mark. "It is useless to think of it. Were I to do so, I should violate the most solemn pledge that a man can give."

Miss Brush was silent. She sat for a few minutes. "Then I go back as rich as I came," said she, at last, while something like a tear glistened in her hard eye. "Come here to me, child."

"Go, my love," said Mark, as Rosy hesitated. "Go and kiss Aunt Adela."

Adela again took Rosy's hands, and gazed at her long and earnestly. "So you will not come with Aunt Adela?" said she. "You will leave her to go back all alone to her lonely house, with no one to care for her, while you stay with these people, who are no relation to you?"

Rosy looked distressed. "I am very sorry for you, Aunt Adela," said she. "I can't leave my papa and mamma and dear little brother Johnny; but I will write to you, Aunt Adela. I can write letters now. Shall I, papa?"

"Surely, my dear, if Aunt Adela wishes it."

"No," said Miss Brush, abruptly: "what

would be the use? Better forget all about her, if I can." She still held the child and looked at her; then, disengaging one hand, she took from her side a very handsome gold watch, with its accompanying chain and trinkets. "Here, child, take this, and, when you are old enough, wear it. There, now: go to your mother."

She kissed Rosy two or three times, and then set her down.

"I may as well go," said she. "Mark Campion, I believe you have done what you thought right. You have treated me with more forbearance than perhaps I had a right to expect. Veronica, I thank you for your hospitality. Good-morning."

Miss Brush threw herself back in the carriage, and said nothing for some minutes.

"So ends my dream," said she. "I was a fool to entertain it."

"Mark Campion is a singular person," said the lawyer. "Many people think him a man of no force of character, because he is so gentle and easy in his manners and so ready to give up to others; but touch him upon the side of principle, and you might as well try to overturn that court-house. But did not your sister-in-law leave another daughter?"

"I understood the other child died."

"I think **not**. She was adopted by Mr. John Campion, and was certainly alive a year ago. I distinctly recollect seeing her at John Campion's funeral. I never saw a child of her age show such deep grief."

"And where is **Mrs. John Campion**?"

"She is, or was lately, in **New York**. She removed thither after the death of her husband, in order to be near her own friends. She was a Miss Holley."

"Not Anne Holley?"

"Yes: I think her name is Anne."

"I remember Rose spoke of her aunt Anne," said **Miss Brush**.

"Anne Holley! That is another matter. Can you find out her address for me?—quietly, you understand."

"Easily," said the lawyer. "It is only to ask Mr. Clarendon, Mr. Campion's executor."

"Do so, then, at once. Anne Holley!" repeated Miss Brush, again. "That is quite another thing."

CHAPTER XIII.

KITTY.

"SO ends the war of the Rose,—not the war of the Roses," said Mark. "I am glad she went away feeling more kindly towards us."

"I cannot help being very sorry for her," returned Veronica.

"I do not know why you should help it, my love. She is much to be pitied, and not the less that her present position is in a great measure her own fault. As Rosy says, she should have kept her when she had her."

"I wonder why she didn't," said Rosy. "Papa, was I really born in her house?"

"Yes, my dear. As Nelly says, there is a story to it,—a story which I do not care about telling you at present."

"But it was kind in her to give me this beautiful watch," said Rosy, who liked to think well of every one. "See, mamma: it is a great deal handsomer than Aunt Anne's. See all this green on the back, and these little shining stones. Isn't that a letter, mamma?"

"Yes,—the letter B. It is indeed a splendid present," said Veronica, admiring the watch, which was one of the most beautiful of its kind.

"I wish I could wear it," said Rosy.

"Little girls do not wear watches; but you may have it in your room and keep it going. I will lend you my beautiful china watch-stand with the glass shade; and you may wear the chain sometimes, to remember Aunt Adela. Poor thing! I wish we could have done something for her."

"If you could only have persuaded her to adopt one of the children at the 'Home,'" said Mark, smiling. "That would have been killing two birds with one stone."

"I am afraid it would be killing in good earnest," said Veronica. "Unless she is more altered than I have any reason to believe, I should not like to be the one who should put an orphan child into her hands. By the way, was it not odd that she should have said nothing at all of Kitty? She can hardly have forgotten the child's existence."

Q

"Becky told me that, from some words she let fall to her, she thinks Miss Brush believes the child dead," said Mark. "Becky did not undeceive her,—for which I am not sorry."

"You surely cannot imagine that Anne would let Kitty go?" asked Veronica.

"Hardly; but Miss Brush might cause her a great deal of annoyance, especially as Kitty is so discontented with her present position. The poor child is fully persuaded that all her troubles arise from the fact that Anne is not her own mother."

"Well, I cannot help being glad Aunt Adela has gone," said Rosy. "I felt all the time as if she would carry me off before I knew it. I was afraid to go out and pick up Mrs. Grimes's ball when it fell out of the window, that day I was at the Home."

It soon appeared that the shock to Rosy's nerves had been a more serious one than anybody supposed at the time. She had always been a remarkably fearless child; but she now became afraid to sleep alone, afraid to go out by herself, or even to stay alone in the next room to her mother. She was tormented by alarming dreams, and showed a tendency to nervous twitches and starts, which frightened

Veronica. She consulted Dr. Woodman, and made him acquainted with the circumstances.

"There is no use in giving the child medicine," said he. "What she wants is a diversion. Give her, if possible, an entire change of air and scene: take a long journey, or go to the sea-side with her. Any thing to break up associations and give her new ideas. Don't let her sleep or stay alone, if she is timid about it. Let her have a light in her room, if she wants one, and somebody to sit with her till she goes to sleep. You need not be afraid of spoiling her."

"I am not," said Veronica, smiling. "I do not think well-governed children are easily spoiled by indulgence. Do you think it well to talk to her about the unreasonableness of her fears?"

"I should say not. Better let her forget them if she can. It is not her judgment that wants convincing, but her nerves that need putting to rights. I don't think any permanent mischief has been done yet; but it would be very easy to do a great deal. One fright such as might be given her by putting her to sleep alone and in the dark, and her health, and very probably her mind, are ruined forever."

"I would never subject any child to such discipline," said Veronica. "I think it barbarous in the extreme. I have too vivid a recollection of the terrors of my own childhood, to trifle with the fears of a child."

"So much the better for the children you have to deal with," said the doctor. "To hear a great many people talk, and see the way they deal with children, one would think they had come into the world full-grown, in a state of sinless perfection, and having all the arts and sciences at their fingers' ends. Such people always expect children to behave much better than they feel any call to do themselves."

"What do you think of the doctor's plan, Mark?" asked Veronica, as she repeated it to him. "Can we compass it, do you think? You know it will involve taking the baby and Becky; and that will be an expensive proceeding."

"We *must* compass it; and so we will conclude that we can," said Mark. "I think the change will be good for all of us. Suppose, now we are about it, we make a bold plunge, and take Johnny and Rosy down to Maine to see Grandmamma Speedwell? She has never seen either of the children, and we have made her but one short visit since our marriage. That will combine the advantages of the long journey, the entire change, and the sea-side, and Rosy will find so many new aunts, uncles, and cousins that she will forget poor Aunt Adela."

"I should like it very much indeed, if you think it prudent," said Veronica. "Dear grandmamma is eighty-four years old; and, hale and vigorous as she is, I always feel as though every summer might be her last."

"Then we may consider the plan as settled,—at least as far as it can be without consulting Becky. We must take her into our counsels."

Becky consented to the plan, with no more than the expected amount of grumbling and objection-making. It was plain that whatever was done for Rosy must be done quickly; for the child was losing strength and flesh every day. In the course of a week Aunt Phebe Ray was established as housekeeper in South Avenue, and the whole family were on their way, by easy stages, to the small village upon the coast of Maine, where Grandmamma Speedwell was spending the happy and peaceful remnant of her life, the centre of a large and loving circle of children and grandchildren, down to the third generation.

The excellent author of those not-half-appreciated books, "The Week" and "A Peep at my Neighbours," somewhere remarks that no person can be an old disciple without having first been a young disciple. **Grandmamma** Speedwell was an old disciple of more than seventy years' standing. She had given herself to God so early in life that she could hardly remember when she did not love him, and through all her long and varied pilgrimage, through storm and sunshine, light and darkness, she had lived to him with a single-hearted steadfastness of purpose which had saved her many of the pangs and conflicts endured by half-hearted Christians,—those who are always striving to get as much of the world as is consistent with serving God at all. She had received a good education, to begin with, and she had never permitted her mind to rust,— never allowed herself to think that she was too old to interest herself in any thing which interested others. At eighty-four she was still in possession of all her faculties, and the chosen friend and confidant of all the younger people about her, from the son who commanded a mighty East-Indiaman, to the great-grandson who was making his first venture in navigation with a chip and a feather; and for all she had intelligent sympathy, encouragement, and comfort under trouble.

The Speedwell family for generations had taken to the water like ducklings, **and their** houses were depositories of all sorts of marine curiosities and foreign productions, especially from China and the Indies. Among these Rosy wandered at will, admiring, questioning, hearing from uncles and great-uncles wonderful legends of sea and land, and loaded with presents and curiosities. The third generation of Speedwells ran mostly to boys; and, Rosy being the only little girl of the tribe, she was petted and caressed in a way that would have been ruinous to a less thoroughly disciplined child. Even Rosy was sometimes thrown a little off her balance, and showed signs of wilfulness and self-conceit which had seldom been seen in her before.

"Never mind, my dear," said Grandmamma Speedwell, to whom Veronica was regretting some of these manifestations. "It is no more than was to be expected. You cannot always keep the child in a glass case. Sooner or later she must go out into the world and meet the world's temptations. All you can do is to correct the faults as they appear; and caution is necessary even in that, lest in rooting up one fault you may plant others which will be worse than the first. Such corrections sometimes turn out like Nathan's weeding in his father's young strawberry-bed the other day. He got up all the weeds, without doubt: only, he weeded up all the strawberry-plants as well."

"If one could only have some plan to guide one," said Veronica.

"I know of no plan which will answer on all occasions, since no two children are alike, and the same child varies almost from hour to hour. There are a few great *principles;* but no general rule can be laid down for their application, that I know of."

"And what are those principles, grandmamma?"

"Steady, reasonable authority, which allows no margin for fretfulness and uncertainty; perfect sincerity in dealing with children; and the golden rule of doing to others as you would be done by in the same position. These, I think, are the great principles of government;

but their application must be influenced by circumstances."

"I think that last rule—that of doing to children as you yourself would be done by—is one often lost sight of by older people," said Veronica. "Even people who are ordinarily well bred often seem to think that the rules of good manners do not apply to children. They expect the child to say, 'if you please,' and 'thank you,' to them; but they never think of saying so to the child."

"Exactly," said grandmamma, smiling. "I noticed the involuntary face of disgust that Rosy made up, the other day, when Aunt Eunice helped her to pudding with her own spoon. Eunice would have sent one of the children away from the table—and rightly, too—for such a breach of good manners; yet she did it herself without a thought. We see the same thing every day in the way children's amusements and possessions are interfered with by their elders."

"Very true," said Veronica. "I have continually to stand between Rosy and Becky in that respect. Becky is extremely fond of the child, but her ruling passion is order. I made her understand very early in our acquaintance that she must not interfere with Mark's desk or my work-basket, however untidy they might appear in her eyes; but every now and then comes a complaint from Rosy that Becky has burned up all the papers she had to dress her doll with, or hidden her box of buttons, or put her play-drawer in order so that she cannot find any thing. Becky loves neatness above all things; and she does not comprehend that Rosy's bits of coloured paper and strings of buttons **and hoards of** odds and ends are as valuable to the child as her own piece-bag and multifarious balls of yarn and worsted are to herself."

"I know of nothing which interferes more entirely with the comfort of a family, nothing which is more belittling to the person concerned, than that same passion for excessive neatness," said Grandmamma Speedwell. "We used to have, and indeed have still, an exemplification of the effect of this mania, in the person of old Mrs. Moreley—I don't know that you remember her, Veronica?"

"Oh, yes," replied Veronica. "I recollect the reply her little boy made when asked what he would do if his mother died: 'I'd go up the front stairs every day,' said he, promptly."

"Exactly; and it was quite evident that the boy would have looked upon his mother's death as a relief. I do not hesitate to say that Mrs. Moreley has destroyed her influence over her children, ruined the peace of her family and the health of her daughters, and embittered the last days of her husband's life, by her love of neatness and order. He was one of the loveliest and gentlest of Christians; but more than once I have seen the colour rise to his pale cheeks and the tears to his eyes when scolded by his wife for the spots on his clothes and on the floor, caused by the food dropped from his feeble, trembling hands. The boys had no more use of the house than though they were strangers. Every possession of theirs, not absolutely necessary, was, however precious to them, unceremoniously bundled into the fire. No in-door amusements could be permitted, because they littered up the house. Annie's eyes were irreparably ruined, and Julia's spine injured for life, before they were eighteen,—the one by sewing in a room always darkened to keep out the flies, the other by scrubbing and carrying heavy pails of water while she was growing fast. Mrs. Morely has been a member of the church for many years; she dresses in the plainest manner, and probably never went to a place of amusement in her life. Doubtless she would be much surprised to be told that she is a thoroughly worldly woman; and yet her heart is even now as much bound up in the things of this world as that of any fine lady who goes to Saratoga or Newport with sixty dresses in her trunks."

"Where does she live now?" asked Veronica.

"Alone in her own house. She has tried the experiment of living with each of her children in turn; but none of the daughters-in-law are neat enough for her, and Julia's husband will not have her. Julia has married well, and has a large family of children; but Mr. Crosby declares that grandmother spoils all the comfort of the household, and that he will not have his children's temper ruined by her perpetual interference and fault-finding. And really, my dear, I cannot blame him."

With so many objects to divert her mind, and the salt air and sea-bathing to build up her body, Rosy soon recovered from her nervous disorder, and was as healthy and cheerful as ever. The family remained on the coast till the beginning of cool weather in the fall, and returned home by way of New York, to visit Anne and Kitty.

Anne was still living in her boarding-house; and, though she retained her deep mourning, the crape and bombazine had assumed a certain jaunty air very different from that of their earlier days. She received her friends with a curious mixture of cordiality and embarrassment. Kitty was not to be seen, and Veronica naturally supposed she was at school.

"Will not Kitty be able to take a holiday while Rosy is here?" she asked, by-and-by. "It is a long time since the children have been together."

The embarrassment of Anne's manner increased: she coloured scarlet, and she seemed to find a difficulty in replying to the question. A thought flashed across Veronica's mind, but she rejected it as absurd, and waited, in some surprise, for an answer.

"Why, I can't say," stammered Anne; and then, recovering her voice, "The fact is, Veronica, Kitty is not with me at present, and I know very little about her. She has gone South, to her father's friends."

"Not with Miss **Brush**?" exclaimed Veronica, at once enlightened, but hardly able to believe. You have not let Adela Brush take Kitty home with her? Oh, Anne! I could not have believed it."

"I don't know why you should say that, Veronica," said Anne. "Adela was her own aunt, and had the best right to her. She was no relation to me; and I don't see why I was to be burdened with her always, because I took her in when she had nowhere else to go."

"Only that you made a solemn promise to her dying mother to keep her as long as she lived, and, above all, never to put her into the hands of Adela Brush," said Veronica. "I should think you would have remembered the look and tone with which poor Daisy said, 'Bind her out to a trade, send her to an asylum, —do any thing to her,—rather than give her into the power of her aunt Adela.'"

"No one minds promises to sick people," said Anne. "One treats them like children:— any thing to keep them quiet. Adela convinced me that Daisy's version of the story was altogether exaggerated, if not false."

"You know Adela of old to be such a truthful person!" said Veronica, bitterly.

"Oh, well, no doubt she has improved since then. And, besides, to tell you the plain truth, Kitty had grown so naughty and disagreeable that there was no living with her,—at least, I could not live with her,—and I was glad to turn her over to some one with more authority. I am sure the annoyance and mortification I have suffered with that child, no one would believe. There was no trusting her out of sight. She would promise in the most serious way to go straight to school, and then I would find out that she had been playing in the street all the morning."

Veronica remembered Anne's principle, "Nobody minds a promise to a child."

"She would not mind me in the least," continued Anne. "I might call her a dozen times, and she would never come till I had my hands upon her. She regularly answered me back when I reproved her; and if I found the least fault or did any thing she did not like, the first thing was, 'I don't love you, mamma. You are as ugly as you can be.'"

"Yes, I remember she used to say that when she was only three years old," said Veronica, unable to suppress the remark. "I told you then such speeches would not sound as well when she was nine or ten."

"Oh, yes, of course you told me so," said

Anne, in her old, peevish tone. "No doubt you think it is all the fault of my management."

Veronica did not contradict her. She certainly did think so.

"Come; you may as well have it out," continued Anne, as though determined to have a quarrel at any rate. "Come; say on. You think I have done very wrong."

"If you had made up your mind to cast off the child you had adopted, why did you not speak to me?" asked Veronica. "I would gladly have taken her, with all her faults on her head, rather than have her delivered over to the tender mercies of Adela Brush."

"That was just what Adela said," retorted Anne. "She made me promise not to say any thing to you about the matter till she was gone, because, she said, you were so prejudiced against her you would give her no peace. I know you think I am a perfect monster, Veronica: so you might as well say so."

"It will be a terrible shock to Rosy," said Veronica, determined not to quarrel if she could help it. "She had so counted on seeing her sister."

"Well, but now tell me, Veronica," continued Anne, with her old persistence: "do you think that I did so very wrong, after all?"

"I do," replied Veronica. "Since you will have my opinion, Anne, I think you have been very wrong. You have been guilty of a breach of trust."

Anne began to cry. "I am sure I didn't know what to do," she whimpered. "I could not live with her any longer. I suppose you will say that was my fault, too?"

"I think so," said Veronica. "You spoiled her by mismanagement, and then, when the mismanagement produced its legitimate fruits, you turned her off. You would not believe me when I told you that you were ruining the child by allowing her to be disobedient and impertinent when she was small, and that the same faults would be intolerable by-and-by. I must say, I think you have incurred a fearful responsibility, and one that you will have to answer both to the mother of the child and to her Father in heaven. I cannot guess what Mark will say."

Anne was evidently very uncomfortable in her own mind. She had yielded to the temptation to get rid of Kitty, led partly by the real annoyance she experienced from the child, partly by Miss Brush's flatteries,—for, warned by experience, Adela had gone to work much more skilfully with Anne than with Veronica. But her conscience had all the time been uneasy, and since Kitty was gone she had missed her more than she had supposed possible. With all her talent for self-deception, she could not deny the truth of Veronica's words; and she would have given a good deal to get Kitty back again.

The visit was an uncomfortable one on all sides. Mark could not conceal his stern displeasure,—all the more effective from its contrast to his usual gracious kindliness. Rosy was inconsolable for the loss of her sister, and Veronica almost feared the shock to her feelings would undo all she had gained. She took an opportunity to question Jane about the matter.

"Did Kitty go willingly?"

"Well, ma'am, she did and she did not. At first she was rather pleased with the notion of going with Aunt Adela; but as soon as Miss Brush began to try and govern her, which she did directly, Kitty began to dislike her."

"But at the last, Jane?"

"Well, ma'am, it was a curious time as ever

I saw. You must know that Mrs. Campion has a great dread of a scene: so she told Kitty she was not to go till the next day, and went out, pretending she was going to buy her something. When the carriage came, Kitty refused to go till mamma came home. Miss Brush laughed, in that hard way she has,—enough to make one hate her, I am sure, if there was nothing else,—and told her that mamma, as she called her, had gone out on purpose to get rid of saying good-by! You never saw any thing like that child's face, ma'am. She stopped crying as if she had been struck dumb. She turned as pale as death, and just walked down-stairs and got into the carriage without another word. Oh, it was a wicked thing to send her away, Mrs. Campion! To be sure, she was troublesome,—that can't be denied; but it was the training made her so. She was as good as Miss Rosy to begin with. And as to telling the truth, I don't know how she was to learn, when her own mamma never told the truth to her. She didn't, ma'am. She used to promise things and to threaten things that she never meant to do; and the child soon found her out."

"Of course," said Veronica.

"I could not bear to have her go," continued Jane. "It seemed just like selling her for a slave. I did take the liberty of writing to you, ma'am; but, not knowing that you were away, I directed to Milby."

"No doubt the letter was sent on to Bayport after we left," said Veronica. "I would certainly have taken the child myself, rather than have her go so far away from us all. But it is done now, and all we can do to help poor Kitty is to pray for her to that God who is the Father of the fatherless and the Friend of the friendless."

CHAPTER XIV.

MISS BROWN.

"I HAVE heard two pieces of news to-day, Veronica," said Mark, as he came in from the garden and put on his dressing-gown and slippers.

"Not very agreeable ones, I should say, to judge from the extra energy you bestowed upon the uprooting of those bean-vines," said Veronica.

"Not altogether, I must confess; and yet I have no right to be offended,—at one of them, I mean; for the other is entirely agreeable."

"I know the first, I am pretty sure," said Veronica.

"Anne is going to be married!"

"Precisely," replied Mark, surprised. "But how did you know it? Is it town-talk already?"

"Not that I know of. I guessed it long

ago,—while we were there. I don't mean that she was engaged then, but she was thinking about it. She showed it all over her. But who is the happy man?"

"A Mr. Van Dunker."

"What a name!"

"Immensely aristocratic, I assure you. He is some years younger than she is, a young 'man about town,' and, to judge from his picture which she sent to Mr. Clarendon, very handsome and good-natured-looking."

"And I suppose he will spend all her money as fast as possible."

"No: John took care of that. If she marries again, she is to have only the income of her property for life, and at her death it is divided,—one-half to whatever children she may have, the rest to his own family."

"Some people would wonder that you should object to the marriage, that being the case," said Veronica.

"I have no right to object, aside from that. Anne is certainly old enough to know her own mind, and I believe Van Dunker is a very decent sort of young man, as young men go; but I do think she might have waited till the two years were up. It seems an insult to John's memory. I suppose all this accounts for her willingness to dispose of poor Kitty."

"Partly, perhaps, but not altogether. Anne grew very tired of her charge, and she had not patience or sense of duty to enable her to bear with the consequences of her own mismanagement. It was a most cruel thing. I never can think as well of Anne as I did before. I never had any great opinion of her wisdom, but I did not think her so heartless. She might at least have given us the refusal of the child; but there her jealousy came in. Poor Kitty! I would give a great deal to know how she gets on in her new home. I fear she will have some sad times. Adela has evidently high notions of arbitrary government, and Kitty has never been subjected to even a reasonable authority. But what is your other piece of news?"

"Oh, I forgot it! Miss Brown's brother has come home."

"No! Not the real East Indian nabob?"

"Even so: though he does not appear to me to be any great things of a nabob. He seems a plain, sensible kind of man, I should judge, with some little temper of his own, but quite attractive in appearance and manners."

"What account does he give of his long silence?"

"He has been up-country, in the indigo business, living quite among the natives, and seldom hearing any news. He says he has written and sent remittances to his sister again and again, but, hearing nothing, he concluded she was dead. At last some chance took him to Singapore, where he met Charley Stephens and his wife, and they told him his sister was still alive when they left home. Upon that he took a sudden start and came home to see her; expecting to find her as he left her,— living in her own house in comfort. He seems to be greatly shocked at the state of things, and, I imagine, treated Martha and her husband to any thing but an agreeable scene. I can readily conceive his wrath might be rather terrific."

"I am glad of it, with all my heart!" said Veronica. "How did you come across him?"

"He came to the office to see Clarendon, and found only me. I remembered him on the instant; for he was one of my heroes when I was a boy, and he has changed wonderfully little, all things considered. We had a long talk, and I have asked him to dinner to-morrow. I thought we might have his sister to meet him."

"To be sure we will, and Dr. and Mrs. Courtland," said Veronica, heartily. "The doctor will delight in him. I would have given something to witness the scene between him and the Jameses. I wonder what Miss Brown will do?"

"Oh, he has not come home to stay. He talks sensibly enough about that, I think. He says all his interests are in India; it is his home, and he has no other intention than to return and end his days there. His only care is about his sister. He seems much distressed at finding her the inmate of a charitable institution, and talks of establishing her in a home of her own."

"He had very much better leave her where she is, in my opinion," said Veronica. "She cannot be so comfortable anywhere else."

"So I told him; and he admitted that she seemed very well off; but it is the charity which seems to stick in his throat."

"And naturally enough, too; but it would be easy to obviate that," remarked Veronica. "He could give what he pleased to the Home, on the condition that it should be considered an equivalent for his sister's board and lodging."

"There spoke all the managers in one breath," said Mark, laughing.

"But is it not a good idea?"

"Seriously, I think it is, my love; but of course all will depend on Miss Brown's feelings. She may prefer a change."

"As far as my influence goes, I shall use it to keep her where she is. I do hope Martha James will not persuade her aunt to go back and live with her."

"She will gain nothing if she does," said Mark. "Captain Brown told me he was determined to do nothing towards such an arrangement as that."

"Well, I shall see her to-morrow and find out all about the matter," said Veronica. "I must go and tell Becky."

"Becky, did you ever know Captain Brown, Miss Brown's brother, who went to India so many years ago?" Veronica asked the question while she was busy over her preserved quinces, and, surprised at receiving no answer, she looked up. Becky was elaborately ironing one of Rosy's white frocks, and did not seem to have heard. Veronica repeated the question.

"Yes, I know him," said Becky, briefly. "Why?"

"He has come home," said Veronica. "Mr. Campion saw him to-day, and he is coming here to-morrow." She paused, astonished at the effect of her words. Becky, who rarely showed emotion of any kind, had dropped her iron, and was leaning back against the wall, as white as the muslin under her hands. "Why, Becky!" she exclaimed. "What is the matter?"

"Never mind," said Becky, recovering her composure with a violent effort. "I am a fool: that's all. Yes, I used to know him; but I dare say he has forgotten all about me long ago. Well, I might as well tell you all about it," she added, presently. "**We kept** company once, before he went away for good; but some evil tongues came between us. He was jealous, and I was proud; and so we quarrelled, and there was the end of it all. It was more my fault than his: that was one comfort."

Veronica quite understood what Rebecca meant. She said no more, but in her heart she wondered whether it was quite the end. She made up her mind that at least it should not be her fault if Captain Brown did not find out that his old sweetheart was alive and single.

The next morning she went round to the Home in good season. As she tapped at Miss Brown's door, she heard within a voice she knew right well, partly whining, partly coaxing. "So here you are, my lady?" said she to herself. "Just as I expected; but you shall not gain your end, if I can help it."

Martha James was planted in one of the arm-chairs directly in front of the fire, evidently considerably excited. Miss Brown sat knitting in her usual place, calm as usual, but with a certain gentle, inflexible expression about her mouth which her friend took for a good omen. Veronica kissed her, and wished her joy.

"Yes, I am greatly favoured," replied Miss Brown. "I had so long ago given up my brother as dead, that he seems to me like one returned from another world. I found myself questioning, this morning, whether it was not a dream, after all; and I did not feel quite sure till I saw Nathan taking his coffee opposite to me at my own breakfast-table."

"Yes, it is very nice," said Martha. "Only,

I do wish, as dear uncle has stayed away so long, he had just waited a week or two longer, till we got aunt nicely settled at home again. You see, Mrs. Campion, the children are older now, and out of the way, and we have been thinking for some time, Tom and I have, how much we should like to have dear aunt back again to live with us. She would be so much better off."

"I do not at all agree with you," said Veronica. "I think she is much better where she is; and besides, Mrs. James, what becomes of the two hundred dollars you paid into the Home?"

"I suppose they would give it back, of course."

"Not at all, I assure you. Your aunt has boarded it out long since."

Mrs. James winced; but, after all, she concluded that she must venture a small fish to catch a large one.

"Well, perhaps that is so; though two hundred dollars is a great deal to board out. But, as I said, it is a great pity that we could not have had it all arranged before uncle came."

"It certainly is," observed Veronica, with a contempt she did not try to conceal,—"since some people might say that, after neglecting your aunt for eight years, you have only taken her up again because her rich brother has unexpectedly turned up."

"They will have no occasion to say any such thing," said Miss Brown.

"That's just what I think," interrupted Martha, eagerly. "Nobody but scandal-mongers and story-tellers would ever think of such a thing."

"They will have no occasion," pursued Miss Brown, quietly,—"simply for the reason that I have no intention of making any change. I have been here, as you say, Veronica, for eight years, and have been treated with uniform kindness. I have made friends whom I love. I am able to be useful to others, especially to the little ones in the other part of the house."

"I am sure you might be useful in teaching my children, if that is all," again interrupted Martha. "That is one of the things we thought about. I mean," she stammered, seeing Veronica smile, "I meant——"

"I understand you perfectly, Martha," said Miss Brown. "But my mind is made up. I shall never move again, unless the shelter of this roof should be denied me. I have told my brother of my decision; and, after talking it over, he quite approves of it. As to your children, I can do them quite as much good here as in your own house, and probably more, since when I have them by themselves **I am able to control** them, which **I could** never do at home. There is no use in saying any more, Martha," she continued, as Martha opened her lips to reply. "I came here to please you, but I remain to please myself."

"And you are right," said Veronica. "I am very glad you have decided so wisely, and that your brother sees it as you do."

"Just like **you**, Mrs. Campion!—always interfering!" said Martha, beginning to cry. "It is too bad! and when I have told ever so many people, too, that aunt was coming back to live with us; and Tom has gone down town to buy new paper and carpets and all, he was so sure."

"You should not have been in such a hurry to count your chickens," said Veronica.

"Martha, not another word," said Miss Brown; "at least, not upon this subject. I heartily wish you had never brought it up, both for your sake and mine; but say no more. Rest assured that I shall always be ready to do all in my power to help you and your children; but this I cannot and will not do. Say no more."

"I shall say what I please," retorted Martha. "I will never give it up till I tease you into it."

"If that is your determination, I shall give orders not to have you admitted," said Veronica. "I will not have your aunt disturbed by any such importunity."

"We shall see," retorted Martha, with a toss of her head. "You a'n't the only person in the world, Mrs. Campion,—if your husband did write a book."

Veronica only laughed; and Martha finally took her departure.

"You do not know how glad I am to find you so decided in this matter," said Veronica. "I was very much afraid you would be persuaded to go away; and I do not feel as though we could spare you from the Home."

"I shall never leave the Home, so long as I am permitted to remain here," replied Miss Brown. "It has been indeed a Home to me. For Martha's own sake, I would not go to live with her. I know how soon it would be the old story over again. Moreover, I can be more useful to the children here than though I lived in the house with them. At home they are utterly ungoverned. They used to invade my room at all hours, and any attempt on my part to control them was always bitterly resented by their mother, and visited upon me in a way to make me miserable for days together. Here in my own home I can entertain them in such a way as to make it agreeable for them to come, and the being sent home is a penalty they do not like to incur: so I can keep them in very good order. It is singular how much more they think of me, now that I am in a position to command their respect."

"I dare say," said Veronica. "Is not the oldest girl in rather a bad way as regards health? I see her in Sunday-school; and I should be very sorry to notice those pink-and-white cheeks and clear eyes upon any child of mine."

"She is being regularly sacrificed,—killed by inches!" said Miss Brown, sighing. "Jenny was allowed to run wild till she was about thirteen. She was never taught to work, or to employ herself in any way within-doors, but permitted to run as much as she pleased out of school: indeed, she almost grew up in the street. Her lessons in school were a mere farce; as how could they be otherwise, when we consider that there were in her school-room no less than sixty little children from six to ten years old? At twelve she could not read as well as your Rosy did when she was six. Well, about two years ago Martha and Tom all at once woke up to the fact that Jenny was a dunce, —that she was learning nothing at school, and was of less than no use at home. Then, on a sudden, all was changed. Jenny was withdrawn from the public school and sent to Mrs. Martin's, where she was loaded with as many lessons as that lady could be persuaded to give her, besides music-lessons out of school. The girl's own ambition was roused at finding herself associated with those of her own age who seemed so much in advance of her. She was in school from nine till four, and all her evenings were given to her books; and when you know that she had no less than five different studies, besides music and painting, you will not wonder that she had to work late and early to keep up her standing in the school. Just at the most critical time of her life, when she specially needed out-of-door exercise and abundant repose of mind and body, she was overworked in a way that no reasonable person would allow in a young man of twenty in college. As a consequence, her health has broken down; she is subject to all sorts of hysterical affections; she has a constant cough, and is going down the hill that has but one ending, as fast as possible. But Martha is blind. Mrs. Martin herself suggested that Jenny had better be taken out of school; but the only consequence was that Jenny was removed from her establishment and placed in that of Miss Bradley, who ought to have been a cattle-driver, I think," concluded Miss Brown. "She would have exactly suited that position."

"I know her well," said Veronica. "I taught in her school one year. Poor Jenny! I believe a great many girls are sacrificed in the same way. The discipline of mind and body which ought to be spread over at least eighteen years is all crammed into five or six. Perhaps those are the happiest who die in the process, instead of living on in miserable ill health all their lives after. A great many, however, merely turn out dunces. They give the whole force of their minds to resisting the cramming process and trying how little they can learn.

"But, to change the subject, I want you and

your brother to come round to our house to dinner at four o'clock. Now, I shall take no denial."

"Why, you know, Veronica, I never go anywhere; but, this being a special occasion, I suppose I must break through my rule for once. As to Nathan," she added, smiling, "I think it is likely he is at your house now. I happened to mention Rebecca this morning,— perhaps you don't know."

"Yes, I do," said Veronica, much amused. "And so he has found her already? Well, I won't be selfish enough to hope that they will renew their quarrel; though I cannot even begin to guess how I should live without Becky."

On leaving the Home, Veronica called at Dr. Courtland's, and then went round to order certain matters for her dinner-table. As she reached her own gate, she was confronted by a tall, bearded figure, sunburnt and stalwart, just issuing therefrom, and caught a vision of Becky vanishing in the distance. The stranger lifted his hat with an amused sort of conscious expression, and walked rapidly down the street.

"Oh, ho! So you have found your way

round already, have you?" said Veronica. "But I must know more about you before you carry off Becky, if you were the greatest nabob in India. I should like to know how my company-dinner has fared all this time."

CHAPTER XV.

BECKY.

THE company-dinner did not appear to have suffered materially. Every thing was going on as usual in the kitchen. Nelly was helping, as she commonly did upon emergencies, and Becky was elaborating her pie-crust as composedly as though nothing had happened. Veronica glanced at her face, and there indeed was a change. The stern, repressed expression, which she had worn till it had become habitual to her, seemed to have been put away like a mask. She appeared to have grown twenty years younger in a day, and looked again as Veronica remembered her when they first met at Mrs. Campion's on one of Veronica's vacation-visits. Presently Veronica sent Nelly on an errand, and busied herself with something in the kitchen, on purpose to give Rebecca an opportunity of speaking, if she were so disposed. For some little time she worked at her tarts in silence. "Mrs. Mark," said she, finally, "do you believe in answers to prayer?"

"Why, Becky, I hardly see what use there would be in praying unless one did believe in answers," said Veronica. "Where would be the object?"

"Some folks say that the only use is to compose and settle our own minds," observed Becky. "I picked up a book the other day,— I guess it was one of those Mr. Clarendon sent in to be noticed,—which said that it was useless, and even impious, to pray for temporal blessings."

"I do not believe in either view," said Veronica. "I suppose that when God tells us, by his apostle, 'In every thing by prayer and supplication let your requests be made known unto God,' he means just what he says; and therefore I feel at perfect liberty to go to him with all my wants and desires."

"But God does not always give us all we ask him for," said Becky.

"No,—fortunately for us. If I thought God was sure to give me every thing I asked of him, I should hardly dare ask for any thing; but because I have perfect confidence in his infinite wisdom as well as in his unchanging love,—because I believe that he can give me every thing that I desire, and grudges me nothing that is either profitable or pleasant to me,—therefore I am bold to come to him with all my requests, great and small. I do not think there can ever be either danger or presumption in taking our heavenly Father at his word."

"He keeps us waiting a long time, sometimes," said Becky.

"Yes, even till another world, oftentimes, I suspect."

"I am sure I thought that was the way he meant to do with me," said Becky. "Oh, how I have prayed that I might have a chance just to say that I was sorry,—just to set things right! I didn't ask any more than that. Then, when, after all my prayers, I heard he was dead,—oh, it seemed to cut the very ground from under my feet! I was like one lost, for a while. I had always believed that I should be heard,—it seemed as though it must be asking according to his will, to desire to set right what I had done wrong,—and then, I thought, if God denied me in this, what reason have I to think he will hear me in any thing? Oh, it was a dark, dark time! I don't know, now, how I lived."

"It is often hard for us to tell how we lived through the trials we look back upon," said Veronica. "I suppose it is because God has more work for us to do, or because he sees that we are not yet ready to go."

"I suppose he saw that in me," continued Becky; "but I could see nothing,—nothing but darkness. In one way it was good for me. I never understood how I lived upon my trust in God, till that trust was taken away. But, oh, it was a dreary time!"

"And how did the light come, finally?" asked Veronica.

"It came by degrees, without any help of my own," replied Becky. "At first in glimpses, soon lost again. But by-and-by I reflected that this world was not all,—that there was another, where the matter might be set right yet,—that it might be set right already, for all I knew; and somehow, by degrees, I grew quiet again, and was contented to live for the work I had to do, till God's time came. I never looked forward to any thing else in this world,—and don't now, for that matter," concluded Becky, briskly giving a last pinch to her pie, and setting it aside with a decided air, as though it represented something which was altogether finished, and not to be taken up again; "for as to going out to India, and all that, of course it is out of the question, and not to be thought of."

"So it has come to that already, has it?" thought Veronica. "Upon my word, my gentleman has not let the grass grow under his feet." "I would not decide upon any thing hastily, Becky," said she. "Wait a little, and be guided by Providence. You made one serious mistake, it seems, by being in a hurry; don't make another, but pray for direction before you come to a final conclusion."

The days went on, and Captain Brown still lingered, having, as it appeared, got over his hurry to return to India. The more Veronica saw of him, the better she liked him. He had seen a great deal of the world, upon all its sides, and had profited by his experience. He was seriously and unaffectedly religious, full of energy, and earnestly desirous to benefit the people under his employ. Rosy looked upon him as a living story-book, full of lions and tigers, whales and elephants, gotten up for her special edification; and she was inclined to be rather cross with Becky for occupying so much of his time.

"There are the captain and Becky talking out by the gate yet," said she, impatiently, one evening, and peeping between the curtains for the tenth time. "I do wish he would come in. I can't think what they find to talk about so long: can you, papa?"

"I cannot possibly imagine," replied Mark, with a twinkle in his eye; "but have patience, Rosy. I dare say we shall find out some day."

The day came all too soon for Rosy, when she found out what Becky and the captain talked about. Becky was one morning helping Veronica about some necessary rummaging in the garret, where were stored a great many things belonging to Mrs. Campion and Anne. It was a favourable time for confidences. The rain pattered softly upon the roof, the house was all quiet, and Veronica and Becky sat on the floor together, beside a great leather-covered trunk, which had made many journeys from Albany to a neighbouring town, in the days when canals and railroads were not, and Milby itself boasted of only one log hut.

"How these things take one back to old times!" said Becky. "There is a piece of the first French calico I ever had. Mr. John gave it to me, and I thought I was made; for in those days we considered a French calico good enough for any thing."

"Perhaps it would be better for us if we thought so now," replied Veronica. "I often sigh over the days when a pretty delaine was dress enough for any but very extraordinary occasions. Then it was a rare thing to see a silk dress in the street in Milby. But I suppose it is natural for people, as they grow older, to look back and say that the former days were better than these."

"Now, Mrs. Mark, don't you begin to call yourself old," said Becky. "If you do, I shall never have the courage to tell you any thing; for I feel all the time as though I was making an old fool of myself."

"In what particular direction?" asked Veronica, smiling; "and what is it that you want to tell me?"

"Well!—there is that old sampler of mine that I have looked for so often!" replied Becky, holding up the article in question. "I remember how proud I felt when I had worked that picture at the bottom. I mean to give it to Rosy."

"Come, Becky!" urged Veronica. "I know that was not what you were going to say."

"Captain Brown is going back to India next month," said Becky, after another pause, during which her face was buried in the trunk.

"Well," said Veronica, "and he wants you to go with him, I suppose? Is that the secret?"

"Well, yes: I suppose that is the amount of it," said Becky. "But he is not going to stay. He is going to sell out and come back in a little while,—say about two years."

"Oh! and he wants you to wait for him till he comes back?" said Veronica, mischievously. "Well, that will give you a good long time to make your preparations."

"Well, no. You see, we are neither of us as young as we have been, and—and—it would be kind of dreary for him to go all that way back alone; and so,—I do feel real bad about going away and leaving you, Mrs. Mark, that is a fact; but then, you see, it seems as if——"

"As if you owed something to him. Well, Becky, I shall be very sorry to lose you,—more sorry than I can tell; but I do think you have kept the poor captain waiting about long enough."

"And there is another reason for my going, Mrs. Mark," said Becky, eagerly. "There is that poor little Jenny James. Dr. Woodman says that a long sea-voyage and a change of climate would probably save her life. Nathan would like to take her along with him; and of course she can't go without some one to take care of her."

"Of course not," replied Veronica. "And so you mean to take poor Jenny with you. Well, I must say, it is very kind in the captain, after all the provocation the James family have given him. He tells me he has serious suspicions that Tom James appropriated some, at least, of the remittances he sent to his sister."

"The poor girl is not to blame for the faults of her father and mother," said Becky.

"Certainly not. I dare say she will make a very pleasant companion for you. But, Becky, have you considered well? It is a serious undertaking, going so far from home, among strangers."

"And heathens, too! That's the worst of it," said Becky. "I keep thinking of that picture in the London News, of the servants straining their master's coffee through the dirty sock, and apologizing by saying that they never took master's *clean* socks. But then, you see, it was my fault that he went there in the first place; and it is not as if we were going to stay."

"Well," said Veronica, "I shall say nothing against it. I think, with you, that you owe a duty to Captain Brown, and that it is much better for you both that you should be married now than that you should wait longer. I shall not know how to live without you, Becky; but I have no right to require you to make such a sacrifice to me as this long waiting would be. I think you have decided rightly; and I am quite sure that Mark will agree with me."

Mark did agree, and so did Miss Brown, that the marriage had much better take place directly. Rosy alone withheld her consent. She could not see why Becky should want to go clear away to India, among the tigers and snakes, for the sake of that old Captain Brown. She thought him very cruel to take her away, and refused to see any parallel between him and Becky and papa and mamma. Veronica tried to show her that she was selfish in requiring Becky to stay at home for her sake; but Rosy would not be convinced. It was not for her own sake, but for Becky's, that she objected; and she remained to the last wholly unreconciled.

Mrs. James made a great favour of letting Jenny go with Captain Brown, while in her heart she rejoiced in the success of her schemes to worm her daughter into her uncle's good graces. She was very indignant when she heard of the proposed marriage, and talked a great deal of the degradation of such a match; but a hint from the captain silenced her.

"*Your* family, Mrs. James! Pray, who are they, if I may be so bold as to ask?"

Mrs. James coloured with rage; but she said no more.

The wedding was to take place two weeks before the time of sailing. Veronica's sewing-machine ran all day long in Becky's behalf.

The captain produced a gay brocade and a white cashmere shawl, which made his bride the envy of half the ladies in Milby. The wedding took place in church. Rosy so far relented as to act as bridesmaid, in a white muslin frock, and a most wonderful sash, the gift of the bridegroom. Mark gave away the bride, and all went off well.

Jenny James, relieved from school and lessons and delighted with the prospect of her journey, seemed better already, and the doctor prophesied great things for her. They were to go by the way of the Red Sea; and Mark somewhat comforted Rosy by taking her down to New York and on board the ocean-steamer, to see them off.

CHAPTER XVI.

KITTY.

WE must now ask our readers to make a long step, both as regards time and space, in order that we may follow the fortunes of another of our personages. The time is about five years in advance of our last chapter; the place, a large, old-fashioned house in an ancient quarter of New Orleans. In an upper room of this house lies a helpless invalid. It is easy to see that she has no use of her lower limbs, and but little of her hands; while in her face, once handsome, and still striking, but wrinkled and sharpened by pain and impatience, we have some difficulty in recognizing Adela Brush. Who, then, is this in attendance upon her,—this tall, dark girl, so strikingly beautiful, but sad, and wearing a repressed and almost stern expression? Can that be Kitty Campion? Even so.

What a melancholy lot was hers! Assiduous devotion to the necessities and caprices of an invalid, who repaid kindness with reproaches, and self-sacrifice with railing or contempt!

In the hard task of endurance she found an invaluable aid in the faithful Chloe, who on one occasion, when Miss Brush had been unusually petulant, counselled her thus:—

"Never mind, Miss Kitty, honey: don't ye fly out and get angry, whatever she says. You know that's no use."

"I'll try, Chloe," said Kitty. "I do try every day, and I am sorry whenever I answer her back; but she is so awfully provoking."

"That's a fact, she is," answered Chloe; "and I think she's worse now that she has nothing else but her tongue to use. She is, and she always was, the hardest person to get on with that ever I see. I do think, Miss Kitty, ye do 'mazin' well, considerin'. But I'm goin' to get her breakfast ready before I goes up, anyway, and yours too, honey. It's 'mazin' little there is to get, anyhow."

"I am afraid it will be less before long," said Kitty, sighing. "I have no more money; and I don't know where money is to come from, unless I sell something else out of the house; and Aunt Adela won't hear of any thing like that."

"Well, then, honey, you'll just have to take the law in your own hands," said Chloe. "Miss Addy must eat, and so must you. But we needn't take trouble before it comes. The Lord 'll provide."

Now let us return for a season to the North.

Miss Brush had no sooner heard from her lawyer that Rosy had a sister living with her old schoolmate Anne Holiey, than her plans were formed. How they succeeded, we well know. Anne was in truth heartily weary of her charge. Kitty was indeed a trial. Systematically trained from her earliest years to self-indulgence in every form within her reach, allowed her own way in every thing and with everybody, she was at nine years old as haughty, selfish, and discontented as was to be expected. She had become a nuisance of no common order,—there was no denying it; and Anne had neither patience nor principle to enable her to bear with the work of her own hands. Besides, she was meditating the entering into a new relation, in which there seemed to be no place for Kitty. She was easily persuaded that, after all, Miss Brush had the best right to her brother's daughter,—that no doubt poor Daisy had exaggerated her grievances,—that Adela had had great provocation,—that she was just the person, with her firmness, to manage Kitty, and, as she was rich and had no children, it would be for the child's good in the end. In short, she was weary enough of her charge to be ready to get rid of her at the first chance; and here was one ready-made to her hand.

At first, Kitty was pleased enough with the idea of a change. She had got the idea firmly fixed in her mind that all her troubles arose from her position as an adopted child, and she thought an own aunt would be better than a mother who was no mother after all.

She soon found out her mistake; and almost from the first there was open war between them. The journey was one scene of dispute and disobedience; but Miss Brush waited for the grand trial of strength till she should be in her own house. She reckoned without her host. The battle was fought, and Kitty came off conqueror. Headstrong and spoiled as she was, she had one accessible point. She was capable of strong affection for any one who inspired respect in her, and a person she once loved she loved forever afterwards. Unluckily, it was upon this very side that Miss Brush chose to attack her. A few days after their arrival in New Orleans, a visitor asked Kitty her name.

"Catherine Brush Campion," was the reply. It was given without thought, as Kitty had all her life been called by the name of her adopted father; but Miss Brush chose to consider it a direct act of rebellion and a premeditated insult to herself.

"Your name is Catherine Brush, and nothing else," said she, sternly. "Let me never hear the name of that man again."

Kitty's spirit was roused in an instant. "My name is Kitty Campion, and nothing else," cried she, with flashing eyes. "My dear papa was better than any one here; and I will mention his name whenever I please."

"Very well, miss. We will settle that presently," said Miss Brush, grimly. The visitor departed; and then came a terrible scene. Miss Brush insisted that Kitty should promise never to call herself Campion again. Kitty declared she would never call herself any thing else. Miss Brush undertook to chastise her into obedience, and Kitty seized the hearth-broom and dealt her aunt a blow on the face which left its mark for a week.

Finally, when her shrieks had attracted a crowd in front of the house, she was dragged up-stairs by main force and imprisoned in a back garret, where she was kept without food until late the next day. All in vain. Natural obstinacy, wounded affection, and the sense of injustice, combined to support her, and, though she was so faint she could hardly speak, there was unconquerable resolution in the tone in which she answered to Miss Brush's repeated question, "Catherine Brush Campion."

Here was a dilemma! Miss Brush had for once met her match. She dared not keep the child longer without food; but, behold, when food was offered, Kitty would not eat! In fact, she could not. She had fasted just to the point where food was distasteful to her, and she turned from it with loathing. She was put to bed in her aunt's room, and awoke her in the night with a frightful attack of croup, to which she had always been subject. Miss Brush had never seen the disease, and did not know its danger; but Chloe did, and at once despatched a messenger for the doctor. Puzzled at the condition in which he found the child, he questioned those around her, and found out the true state of the case. He was an old family friend, and well knew Miss Brush's character.

"You have all-but murdered the child," said he, sternly. "Exhausted as she is, the chances are a hundred to one against her rallying. Were you mad? Do you want another coroner's inquest in the house?"

"What was I to do?" asked Miss Brush, sullenly. "The child would not obey me. Was I to give up to her?"

"You acted like a fool in provoking a contest upon such a subject," replied Dr. Fuller. "If the battle must come, why not let it come upon some point of real consequence, and not upon one in which all the poor child's affections were engaged? One such piece of injustice and cruelty was enough to destroy your influence with her forever. Suppose you had conquered: what do you think you would have gained? Nothing but the child's undying hatred and distrust."

"I was a fool to have any thing to do with her," said Miss Brush.

"Ay, there I agree with you; but, now you have got her, remember that children are not always to be straightened, like crooked nails, by sheer hammering, and that even in hammering a nail it is necessary to strike in the right place, to do any good."

The struggle was a severe one; but Kitty's good constitution triumphed, and, after twenty-four hours' hard fighting, she was pronounced out of immediate danger. A low fever followed the attack, and it was two weeks before Kitty was able to leave her bed. Now was the time for Miss Brush, in some measure, to undo the harm she had done, and by kindness and attention to gain the child's heart. But no: Miss Brush hated a sick-room. She was no nurse, she said,—which was true enough; and she lacked the unselfish affection which might supply the place of skill. She contented herself with providing every thing the doctor recommended, and coming once or twice a day to stand for a moment at the bedside and ask a few questions, to which Kitty would hardly ever reply. At last she recovered; but Miss Brush never again approached the subject of her name. Conquered once, her pride would not let her risk a second defeat.

For a while Kitty seemed entirely changed. A sullen, brooding dulness appeared to have taken the place of her former vivacity of temper. She hardly ever replied to her aunt's sarcasms, or responded to her rare approaches to something like affection. Miss Brush sent her to school, where she got on tolerably well, considering her bad training. It would be hard to find a more unhappy child than poor Kitty was at this time. She lived in a state of constant hostility to her aunt and to most of her school-fellows. Her teachers could make nothing of her. Miss Brush hated animals of every kind, and would allow no pets about the house; and if the servants smuggled in a kitten or puppy for Kitty's benefit, it was sure to be persecuted without mercy. Kitty had but two friends. One was Dr. Fuller, who had become interested in the forlorn child, and the other was Chloe. With neither of these two could Miss Brush afford to quarrel, and the latter was especially necessary to her in the services required by the increasing but carefully concealed disorder under which she laboured.

As though determined to set pain at defiance, as she had done every thing else, Miss Brush went into company more and more; and the happiest hours Kitty knew were those in which her aunt was away, and she spent the evening with Chloe, hearing her sing her Methodist hymns, reading the Bible to her, and listening

"You've got to love the Lord, and try to please him." p. 299.

to stories about her own mother, and about the aunt Catherine for whom she was named.

"Oh, Miss Kitty, my lamb, if you would only take after her!" Chloe would say. "You'se going to look jest like her; but you haven't got her sperrit, honey. She was as meek as a lamb,—poor dear!" And then Chloe would repeat the story of Catherine's gentleness, of her attachment and engagement, broken off by the pride of her family, of her piety and her early death. "You see, she wasn't afraid to die," she would conclude. "She know'd she was goin' to her Father's house of many mansions, you was readin' about just now; and she was glad to go."

"I wish I was there!" said Kitty, one night. "Then I should see my dear papa Campion."

"Ah, my lamb, but you'se got to be a different child from what you are now," said Chloe. "You'se got to love the Lord, and try to please him and be like him; and you don't do that now. Your poor little heart's full of hatred and spite, and you don't forgive. You hate poor Aunt Adela; and that a'n't the sperrit that was in Christ Jesus. He loved his enemies and died for 'em; and he loves poor Miss Addy, though she hates his very name.

You can't go to heaven while you'se like that, honey. You can't never go to heaven while you hate anybody."

"Then I can't go at all, Chloe; for I can't help it."

"But the dear Lord can help it for you, honey. He can give you the Holy Spirit, and change your heart, so's you'll love what you hated before, and hate what you loved before. He can, my lamb. He did it for me, and I'm sure he will for you." And Chloe proceeded to tell Kitty her own story,—a tale of wrongs too common in those dark days, and which need not be repeated here. "Think of that, my lamb! And if he could do that for me, couldn't he do it for you, that's so much younger and has so much less to get over?"

This was not the first nor the last of such conversations. In one sense, the soil was prepared for the good seed. Kitty's very desolation made her feel the need of a friend. As we have seen, she could love deeply where she could respect; and the character of our Lord, as she read of it in the Gospels, attracted both respect and love. She began to think of him as Chloe did,—as a real, living, always present, all-powerful friend,—and to wish to have him on her side. Then came fierce conflicts. She would resolve and re-resolve to please him and be like him; but the first sneer or sarcasm from her aunt would upset all her resolutions and bring on a fit of anger and rebellion which drove her to despair. Then she prayed for help against her sins, and for pardon; and at last, with Chloe's help, she found the peace which comes from a consciousness of acceptance with God through Christ's atoning blood.

She had a hard time, poor child, after all. The selfish and rebellious habits of her lifetime came back to plague her. She had never been taught any self-control; and it was hard to learn now. Her aunt's sneers and taunts seemed to increase in proportion to her efforts to meet them in a Christian spirit; for Miss Brush was not one to be disarmed by gentleness. But those on Kitty's side were stronger than those against her, and slowly, with many falls and hard bruises, with many conflicts and not a few defeats, she advanced in the way that leads to life.

At last Adela's disease reached a point at which it could no longer be concealed. She was attacked, in addition, by a sort of paralysis, which confined her to her bed and made her entirely dependent upon those about her. She was now to find out the worth of the strong will she had always boasted of as able to sustain her under any trials. She found it could not so much as bring to her lips a glass of water, though it stood under her longing eyes. She was dependent for the very means of existence upon those whom she had always ill treated, and who now had it in their power to repay her with interest. Well was it for her that a stronger hand than hers had been dealing with them, undoing the mischief she had wrought.

Poverty was now added to her trials. Of her servants in New Orleans, some had been sold to supply the pressing needs of the house, some had run away, some had died. At the time our story finds her, there was no one left in her large and stately house but Chloe and Kitty; and neither of them knew where to look for next day's meal. But for Chloe's timely discovery of some coffee, Kitty would have breakfasted on dry bread and water. Piece after piece of silver had been sold, until little remained to dispose of but family jewels, which Adela would not hear of parting with.

CHAPTER XVII.

THE MEETING.

"MISS ADDY'S asleep now," said Chloe, presently coming down to the room where Kitty was still lingering over her cup of coffee. "I think likely she'll have a long nap. You just go and sit by her, and I'll do up the work, and then I'll just curl down and have a sleep myself. I'se powerful sleepy, that's a fact."

"I should think you would be," said Kitty, rising. "You ought to let me stay with aunt part of the night."

"No, honey! You'se young and gittin' your growth, and it a'n't healthy for young girls to be up nights. You does too much as it is."

"If it was only the doing!" sighed Kitty.

"Yes, yes, I know; but don't complain, honey. Take up your cross,—that's the only way."

Kitty went up-stairs, and, finding her aunt still asleep, she sat down by the open window with her Bible, sometimes reading, sometimes looking out upon the silent city and thinking of home. "What had become of them all? Why had Uncle Mark never answered the letters she had sent him? Or had he answered them? What was Aunt Veronica doing? What was Rosy like? Should she ever see them again?" She was roused from her revery by a voice from the bed.

"How anxiously have I sought for happiness in the world! It was a great mistake,—all a mistake! Every thing has been a mistake, all my life long. It might have been different, if—but it is too late now. Do you remember your mother, Catherine?"

"No, aunt," said Kitty, wondering more and more. "She died when I was very little."

"Yes, to be sure. You are not like her. You are like your aunt Catherine. You never heard of her?"

"Yes, aunt: Chloe has told me about her."

"That was another mistake!" continued Miss Brush. "We might have let her marry him and go away. Ah, well! they are both dead now: so it is all the same. Open my Chinese cabinet, child, and give me an ivory box you will see there. Yes, that is it. Now open it. Press your hand on that stud. Harder:—it has not been opened in years and years. Ah, there it goes. Now take out the miniatures and open them. Whose is that?"

"A lady and gentleman, aunt. What a beautiful woman!"

"That is your mother, Catherine. Just so she looked when she came here a bride. Ah, how I hated her! Perhaps that was a mistake too."

"I think it is a mistake to hate anybody," said Kitty. "But why did you hate mamma?"

"She crossed me, child. She would not be guided by me, and she weaned your father from me. He had been under my thumb before that. I thought her a soft little fool, whom it would be easy to govern. She crossed me, and so I hated her. But—I don't know,—perhaps it was a mistake—I had my revenge at last."

"And did that do you any good, Aunt Adela?—the revenge, I mean?" asked Kitty.

"Revenge is sweet, child. Don't you find it so? Don't you rejoice now that you see me helpless, dependent, in your power? Don't cant, but tell me the truth."

Kitty paused a moment. "No, Aunt Adela," she replied. "If I could cure you myself, or if I could bring some one to cure you, as they brought our Saviour to cure the centurion's servant, I would do it in a minute."

"Catherine Brush, lay down that box. Now put your hands on mine. Look me in the face,—so! Now tell me the truth! Don't you hate me? You do, in your soul! Don't you?"

"No, aunt. I did once; but I don't now. I don't love you as much as I should like to; but I do not hate you, and I would help you in a minute, if I could."

Miss Brush looked long and searchingly into her niece's face. "I believe you say true, child. There is no hate in your eyes, and no falsehood. But I don't understand it."

"Aunt Adela," said Kitty, earnestly, "I will tell you how it was,—truly. I did hate you,—so that I would have liked to kill you,—till Aunt Chloe taught me to love God. And when I learned to love Him I left off hating you. I have begun to love you since I have had so much to do for you; and when I am a better girl I hope I shall love you a great deal more."

Kitty's heart warmed with her own words, and, almost for the first time, she stooped and kissed her aunt, with a feeling of real affection.

Miss Brush returned the kiss.

"There, child; I believe you, however you came by it. And, Kitty,"—this, too, was new in her: she had never called her any thing but Catherine, usually Catherine Brush, as if constantly to remind her of their first quarrel,—"and, Kitty, if you can, when I am gone, take care of Chloe. She has been a faithful servant to our house. I can't say any more now. There; put the things away. Stay; let me see the other picture."

Kitty put it into her hand. It was that of a very lovely young woman; and even Kitty could see the likeness to herself.

"That is your aunt Catherine. You are like her. She, too, found comfort in religion. I never had any. There; put them away, or keep them if you like. All the things in that cabinet are yours. There are some jewels. Take care of them. Oh, my child, what is to become of you?"

"Never mind, aunt," said Kitty, wondering more and more. "I shall be taken care of somehow. But, aunt, have you got any money?"

"No, child,—not a picayune."

"Nor have I, aunt; and I don't see what we are to do, unless we sell something more."

"Don't talk about it now," said Miss Brush. "Do what you please,—you and Chloe,—but don't tell me about it. There are some gold chains and a cross and rosary of your grandmother's: I never thought to sell them; but you cannot starve. Take them to Black; he is an honest man; perhaps he will lend you something on them till better times. Kiss me again, Kitty. There; now let me sleep."

Kitty waited till her aunt was asleep, and then she slipped out and went to find Chloe, who listened with awe-stricken interest to her account of her recent interview with her aunt.

"She's changed for death, Miss Kitty," said she, with the superstition of her race. "When folk changes like that, all at once, it's a sure sign the hand of the Lord's on 'em. She won't last much longer. I guess I'd better go for the doctor."

"Perhaps you had; though I don't suppose it will make much difference. I can't think she is dying, Chloe,—she speaks so much more clearly; and she looks better, too."

"It's just the flashing up of the lamp before it goes out, my lamb. You haven't seen as many death-beds as I have. I pray the good Lord you never may. I reckon I'd best run for Dr. Fuller; 'cause, you know, if any thing should happen——"

Chloe went on her errand, but returned unsuccessful. The doctor had gone out into the country to some surgical case, and would not be back for a day or two.

"We must just leave her in the Lord's hands, Miss Kitty. There a'n't nothin' else we can do, as I see."

Miss Brush slept for a long time, and, when she awoke, even Kitty's inexperienced eye could see a great change. She was very quiet, all her usual fretfulness and impatience which made her so hard to manage being gone. She dozed a good deal, and wandered at times, but could always be roused by Kitty's voice, and at such times was quite herself. She seemed to cling specially to Kitty, and was unwilling to have her out of her sight.

The next day, however, it became necessary for Kitty to go out. There was literally no food in the house, and nothing wherewith to buy food. Miss Brush had none but very distant relatives living, and most of them had left town. It would not answer, for obvious reasons, to send a servant to dispose of so valuable an article as the **rosary, upon which** Kitty proposed to raise some money.

It was with some little trepidation that she entered Mr. Black's shop. She had been there before upon a similar errand, and she could never divest herself of a feeling of shame and mortification,—though she told herself over and over that there was no sin in being poor. There was no one in the shop but a gentleman who had his back turned towards her and was busy trying some gold pens.

"My dear Miss Brush, I would gladly accommodate you if I could," said Mr. Black, "but really I have no money. This rosary is a valuable article. The gold is sterling and very old, and the old coins attached are worth far more than their intrinsic value, as curiosities. This one, you see, is of the time of the Roman Empire, and very rare. It would be a pity to part with this **relic unless it is necessary**."

"It *is* necessary," said Kitty, hardly able to restrain her tears at the disappointment. "Unless you can give me something for the whole, I must take off the coins and spend them in the market."

"Will you allow me to look at the rosary?" said a voice which thrilled Kitty through and through; and the gentleman, who had caught the last words of the conversation, stretched out his hand for the beads.

"These coins are, as you say, very valuable," said he. "I will gladly purchase them, and the rosary also, if you will place a price upon them."

He turned smilingly to Kitty. There was no mistaking the clear, dancing blue eyes, the sweet, firm mouth, fringed with a yellow beard and mustache.

"My dear child, I fear you are ill," exclaimed the gentleman, hastily; for Kitty had turned white even to her lips. Kitty gasped for breath, and said, in a sort of hoarse whisper,—

"Uncle Mark, don't you know Kitty?" The next moment she seemed to feel herself caught in a pair of strong arms just as the floor was sinking with her. When she recovered, she found herself upon a couch in the back part of the store, with Uncle Mark bathing her face, and Mr. Black fanning her.

"There! that's better," said Mr. Black,

kindly; "you are coming to yourself, and I will leave you to your friend."

"Uncle Mark, is this really you?" said Kitty, faintly. "I don't know how to believe it."

"Well, Kitty, I never was in New Orleans before, and am somewhat confused myself," said Mark, smiling, "but, so far as I can tell under these strange circumstances, it is myself and no one else. I find it much harder to believe that this tall young lady is little Kitty."

"But I must not stay," exclaimed Kitty. "Aunt Adela has had no breakfast, and she cannot have any till I get home. Uncle Mark, will you really buy the rosary?"

"Certainly, my dear. But, Kitty, has it come to this? Are you straitened for the means of life?"

"Uncle Mark, we have not one thing to eat in the house, except some coffee and brown sugar. I must go and buy something directly." She tried to start up, but sank back, dizzy with fasting,—for she had eaten nothing more than a mouthful of dry bread since the day before at noon.

"Wait a little," said Mark. "Lie still till I come back." He went out, asking a question of Mr. Black in passing, and presently returned with some coffee and crackers,—all he could find at the moment.

"You must eat and drink," said he; "and then we will go to market, if you will show me the way."

"Law bless you, Miss Kitty, honey, what a lot of things you'se sent in!" said Chloe, meeting Kitty at the door. "I ha'n't seen so many pervisions together this many a day. You must be keerful, honey. There's no knowin' where the next money is to come from." Catching sight of Mark at this point, Chloe intermitted her lecture and performed her grandest curtsy.

"This is my uncle Mark, Chloe,—the one I have so often told you about."

"Bless the Lord!" exclaimed Chloe. "Now it'll be all right. Go up to Miss Addy, honey; she's been asking for you. You see, Mas'r Mark," she continued, after Kitty had left the room, "I'se been powerful troubled in my mind what was to become of Miss Kitty when Miss Addy was gone, 'cause there don't seem no one to take charge of her; but the Lord he's made it all right. He allers does. Bless the Lord!"

"You have been a long time away, Kitty," said Miss Brush, feebly. "Where have you been?"

"To Mr. Black's, aunt, and to market. How do you feel?"

"Did you sell the rosary?" asked Miss Brush.

"Yes, aunt, and got a good price. I have bought a large supply of provisions, and I have some money left."

"Take care of it." She was silent, and lay with her eyes closed for a time; then she spoke, with unusual strength and clearness. "Kitty, listen to me. I know I am dying. When I am gone, ask Dr. Fuller to sell what he can of the contents of this house and raise money enough to send you to your friends at the North. I made my will long ago, and left what I had to you. There is no one here to take care of you; but your uncle Mark is an honest man, and will do what he can for you. Go to him."

"Aunt Adela," said Kitty, as she paused for breath, "Uncle Mark is here,—in the house. I met him this morning."

"Bring him here," said Miss Brush. "Bring him here, quickly!"

Kitty hastened to call her uncle; and Mark was soon beside the bed. He saw at once that the end was near.

"Mark Campion, you profess to be a Christian," said Miss Brush. "Are you Christian enough to take this girl, penniless as she may be, and give her a home with her sister?"

"I ask nothing better, Miss Brush," answered Mark, solemnly. "God helping me, she shall never want a home, but shall be to me in all things as my own."

"Good!" said Miss Brush, with evident satisfaction. "Catherine, I have not made you happy. I was not fit for the charge I took upon myself. Forgive me, if you can."

"Indeed I do, aunt!" sobbed Kitty. "I know I was very perverse and naughty. Please forgive me, Aunt Adela."

Miss Brush smiled. "We may call it even, Kitty. Chloe has done far more for you than I. Be kind to her—" Her voice failed.

"She is going!" said Chloe, in an awe-struck tone. "Oh, Miss Addy, honey, look at Jesus!—look at Him, just once, before you go! O good Lord, have mercy on her!"

"It is all over!" said Mark, solemnly. "Come away, Kitty, my love. You have been faithful to death; but you can do no more. She is in God's hand."

CHAPTER XVIII.

REUNION.

"KITTY, what church did your aunt attend?" asked Mark, on the afternoon of the same day. "We must make arrangements for the funeral as soon as it will be decent."

"Aunt Adela never went to church, Uncle Mark," replied Kitty. "She has never been since I came here,—nor I either, except twice to the Catholic cathedral when I went to the Sisters' school. It seemed so strange, when I first came, not to go to church, and to see aunt and her friends playing cards on Sunday evening. It made me more home-sick than any thing else."

"I should think so, indeed. But did you *never* go to church?"

"Never,—only, as I said, two or three times to the cathedral. Aunt Adela said if I must have a superstition I might be a Catholic, as my grandmother was before me; for that was at least venerable and graceful. I believe, honestly, it was what she said, as much as any thing, that set me against it, to begin with; for I hated her so in those days that just the fact of her liking any thing made me hate it. Yes, it was very wrong, I know; but you don't know all I had to bear."

"I can guess, my poor child."

"The nuns were very kind to me, even when I would not go to church," continued Kitty. "I learned a good deal from them,—fine work, and music. Some of aunt's relations came to see her after she was taken down sick, and wanted her to send for a priest; but she would not hear of it, and fairly drove them out of the room. They have not been near us since. I think you had better manage the funeral your own way, Uncle Mark."

"I don't see but I shall have to do so, my dear. I wish, however, that your aunt's physician would return."

Dr. Fuller arrived in the course of the afternoon, and gave Mark a warm welcome. He produced Miss Brush's will, by which Kitty was made her sole heir, with himself for executor and guardian. There were no directions about the funeral; and Mark thought it better to get the matter over as quietly as possible.

The next day but one, Adela Brush was laid in the burying-place of her family.

My story need not be greatly prolonged. The most valuable of Kitty's possessions—the jewels and remaining plate—were packed up and stowed in a place of safety. Mark was able to make an arrangement by which the house was let, furnished, to a quiet, motherly woman, with whom Kitty could board comfortably till Mark was able to take her home. Chloe remained in the house as servant, somewhat puzzled and put out now and then by the lady's particular ways, but happy to be near her dear Miss Kitty. She had now no tie to life but Kitty; and thus, when Mark and his charge sailed for New York in October, Chloe, with many misgivings, made up her mind to accompany them.

"I'se an old woman," said she; "I ha'n't got many years to stay, anyhow; and when the Lord calls me home, it may as well be from the North as from the South. 'Twon't be no further to go from one than from the other, I reckon."

They were obliged to pass a Sunday in New

York; and they spent it with Anne. The visit was rather unwillingly made on Kitty's side. She resented the second marriage as an affront to her father, and she had never gotten over the strong impression made upon her by Anne's heartless conduct at the time of their separation. Poor Kitty's temper was destined to be her great enemy all her life long.

The mother and daughter once brought face to face, however, old associations resumed their sway, and they met with affection on both sides. Anne had much to say upon the subject of Kitty's improvement in person and manners, and took great credit to herself for her wisdom in giving her to Miss Brush.

"I knew she was just the one to manage you, Kitty. She had so much firmness, and I never had: my feelings were too strong. But I always thought you would turn out well,—quite as well as Rosy, for all Veronica's boasting. I never did believe in so much government. I believe in letting nature have her way. You see **now** how much wiser I was in letting you go to your aunt."

The speech was not very consistent; but Anne's thoughts were never remarkable for coherency. Kitty repressed with some trouble the reply which rose to her lips, and turned the conversation by inquiring about Anne's little boy, now some three years old.

"Oh, he is with his nurse. He will be down presently. His nurse is a Frenchwoman, a most superior person, and I leave him almost entirely to her. He can speak more French than English already."

The child presently appeared,—a pale, delicate little fellow, with bare arms and legs, both blue with cold. He took at once to Kitty, and chatted merrily with her in his childish French. Presently he used a very coarse—indeed, indecent—expression.

"Oh, Louis, you should not say that," exclaimed Kitty, much shocked. "That is not proper."

"Nurse says so," returned the little fellow, innocently, and ran on as before, saying, "Mon Dieu!" at every other word.

"You would not like to hear your child swear at that rate in English," Mark could not help saying.

"Oh, but in French,—that is different," said Anne. "All French people say so. It is not the same at all."

"It means exactly the same," said Mark.

The more Anne saw of Kitty, the more she was charmed; and before Sunday evening she coolly announced that she had quite made up her mind to keep her.

"You must see, Kitty, that I have the first claim upon you, now that your aunt is dead. You could be very useful to me, especially in teaching Louis. Your French accent seems so pure; and it would be a great comfort to me to have some one I could depend upon to walk with him, and so on. And I am sure it would be the most natural arrangement."

Kitty compressed her lips, and made no answer. Anne went on urging various arguments, and ended with, "I am sure, after all I have done for you, you must see it your duty to be guided by me."

"And suppose you get tired of me, as you did before, mamma? What will you do then?" asked Kitty, bitterly. "You can't send me to New Orleans this time, you know."

"You could go to Aunt Veronica, if we did not get on well together," answered Anne, simply; "or you could go to school."

"Thank you, mamma," replied Kitty, still more bitterly. "I rather prefer going to Aunt Veronica of my own accord, to being shoved off on her because no one else wants me."

"Kitty, what an idea! But I shall talk to your uncle Mark."

"No, Anne," said Mark, seriously, when Anne proposed the idea to him. "It is not to be thought of. I promised Adela Brush that Kitty should be as my own; and I intend to keep my word. You gave up all claim upon her when you put her into Adela's hands. Adela transferred her **to me**; and I mean to **keep** her."

"Just like you!" said Anne, peevishly. "I suppose you will let the child stay if she pleases?"

"Do you please, Kitty?" asked Mark.

"Do you think I ought to stay, Uncle Mark?" asked Kitty, with a quivering lip. "I would try to do what was right."

"There! I knew she would stay," exclaimed Anne, triumphantly.

"Do you think so, Uncle Mark?"

"No, Kitty, I do not; nor could I give my consent to such an arrangement. You chose me for your guardian when Dr. Fuller died; and I prefer that you should reside under my own roof."

"Oh, very well," said Anne. "I have done. It just proves what I have always said,—that there is no creature so ungrateful as an adopted child."

Kitty burst into tears and ran out of the room; and when Mark sought her he found her sobbing as though her heart would break, while Chloe in vain tried to comfort her.

"Come, Kitty, cheer up. You have done nothing wrong. Mamma will think better of it presently."

"Then you don't think I am obliged to stay, uncle?" said Kitty. "I wish to do my duty; but oh, Uncle Mark, I earnestly desire quiet and rest somewhere."

"And you shall have it, Kitty. Cheer up, my dear. We shall soon be at home and in peace."

I need not describe the meeting between Kitty and her friends. Suffice it to say that she was made welcome with all the love that Rosy and Rosy's mamma had to bestow.

Chloe was installed at once in the kitchen, where a succession of incompetent helps had driven Veronica to distraction ever since Becky went away. She is still living, and, like many coloured people after they reach a certain age, time seems to make no impression upon her. She considers Mrs. Campion needlessly particular upon the subject of dish-towels, and wishes Missus would keep **out** of the kitchen; but, on the whole, they rub along together very comfortably. Rosy is the sunshine of the house, and pours out upon her younger brother and sister all the love which was bestowed upon her own youth.

If Rosy is the sunshine, Kitty is sometimes the storm. **She** still feels the disadvantages of her early training, or want of training,— still has many a battle to fight with selfishness, passion, jealousy, and idleness. But her face is set firmly heavenward, and her progress, on the whole, is in the right direction. She now and then makes Anne a visit; and these visits have increased in length and frequency since little Louis has been such an invalid. The poor child is a martyr to inflammatory rheumatism, the fruit of the "hardening process" he was put through in early childhood; and no one can make him forget his pains and amuse his weary hours like Sister Kitty.

Becky and her captain have at last returned from India and settled near Milby, where they have bought a small farm. Poor little Jenny

James lies in the English burying-ground at Bombay. Miss Brown still survives, the oldest member of the Old Ladies' Home.

Neither Mark nor Veronica have yet had any reason to complain of the ingratitude of adopted children.

"But, after all, what is the great difference?" some reader may say. "You **say** Rosy **and** Kitty are both Christians,—both walking in the narrow way which leads to life: so what is the great difference, after all?" The difference lies just here:

To Rosy the path is made as easy as it can be, by the cultivation in her of lifelong habits of self-control, of self-forgetfulness, of patience and gentleness.

To **Kitty it is in** a manner hedged **up with thorns and** built up with hewn stones, by habits of exactly the contrary kind,—habits of selfishness, jealousy, imperious self-will.

With Rosy the thought **of** pleasing and helping others comes naturally first, by long course of habit; **to** Kitty comes first the thought of pleasing herself, only to be overcome by such a struggle as often makes the service or the sacrifice any thing but a gracious one. In short, the training of the one will be a lifelong help and comfort to her; that of the other will be to her a lifelong hindrance and misery.

If a man sows good seed in his ground, more than one weed will doubtless spring up with it, which it will require care and patience to root out; but if a man sows his ground wholly with tares, or even if he allows the natural weeds of the soil to spring up unchecked, it will require much hard ploughing and hoeing and grubbing to get even a small quantity of good grain to sprout; and, after it has once gained a foothold, it will have a hard struggle to bring ever so little fruit to perfection.

THE END.

www.ingramcontent.com/pod-product-compliance
Lightning Source LLC
Chambersburg PA
CBHW030728230426
43667CB00007B/636